The MATTER of HOPE

Transmuting Significant Life Changes
and Loss Workbook

Alice Molter-Serrano
Creative Communications Circuit

Published by:

C

Alice Molter-Serrano
Creative Communications Circuit
340 Birch Blvd.
Sedona, Arizona 86336

Copyright © 2015 by Alice Molter-Serrano
All rights reserved.
ISBN: 978-0692553169

All rights reserved. No part of this book may be reproduced or transmitted in any form or by any means, electronic or mechanical, including photocopying, recording, or by any information storage or retrieval system without prior written permission from the publisher.

This book is to be regarded as a reference source and is not intended to replace professional advice for physical, emotional, or medical problems with the advice of your counselor or physician. The author and the publisher disclaim any liability arising directly or indirectly from the use of this book.

Cover by David Engle
Photo of Alice pregnant with Hope by Jason Lome
Editing by Jacqueline Guineau
Printed by CreativeSpace
Printed in the United States of America

Dedicated to:

Our sweet daughter, Hope,

She came for an instant
Which will last forever.

Stephen, Our son,

Whose bravery and wisdom
Gave me rebirth and hope.

Acknowledgements

This book has been a long time in coming. Life happens and time goes by and people come and go but the people I would like to thank were instrumental not just with writing of this work but in my life.

Thank you Hope
for coming into this world if only for a moment.
You gave us all Hope just by coming and even upon your departure you taught me what true Hope is after despair. I love you forever.

I want to acknowledge my spouse, soul mate, and father to Hope, Edwin. This work is just as much his as it is mine. I love you very much.

Thanks to a beautiful soul and my son who has endured and stayed strong through rough times. I love you, Stephen.

Thank you Marilyn James for being my friend and for you observation of who I am that led to all of this work.

Deborah Mabingani and Jason Lome, thank you for being present at the time of Hope's birth and being there for Edwin and me.

To my parents, Lucille and Paul Molter for being the rock under my feet, I give thanks.

Thanks to Christina Laurel, Elizabeth Soto, Lisa Townsend, Kathy Powell, Steve Spahn, Lynn Buckner, Zion, Sig and Sarah Hauer, Cheryl Arata, Sarah Roscoe, Dianne Walter-Butler, my sister Sherry, Becky, David, Sunshower, and all my students and clients for your support and encouragement.

And to Jacqueline Guineau, my friend and editor, who not only stood by me in so many moments of grief and hopelessness but also watched me leap to the other side of it all in joy. Thank you!

Contents

Preface: *A Place Called Hope......iv*
    You Deserve to be Happy......x
    Alice Pregnant with Hope......xii
    Song for Hope......xiv

Introduction: *My Story of Hope*

Part I. Our Emotional Body

The Heart of the Matter..............4
The Matter of Fear....................10
The Matter of Anger..................14
The Matter of Humor.................18
Emotional Time and Space........20

Part II. Symbols

My Symbols...............................24
The Four Corners of Hope.........27
Perception and Perspective........32
It Is All in How You Look at It....33
Begin With a Point....................35
The Mandala of Hope................38
Instructions for Making a Mandala...........39
Letting Hope Fly.......................41

Part III. Archetypes and Myths

Myths Can Help Us Heal............44
The Myth of Hope.....................46
The Myth of Life and Death.......48
The Tree of Life........................51

Part IV. Thought As Matter; Our Mind

Thought as Matter....................58
What Were You Thinking?........62
Negative to Positive Thoughts...63
Conscious Living......................65
Brain Gym...............................67

Part V. Spirit As Matter

Sound into Matter.................72
Spirit in Matter.....................74
Meditation As Vibration..........76
Faith...................................77
Synchronicities....................79
Natural Course of Life...........81
Stillness That is You..............82

Part VI. The Matter of Our Physical Body

The Matter of our Body..........88
Breathing.............................90
Physical Effects of Loss..........93
Our DNA: the Key to Hope......94

Part VII. Nature

Our Physical World................106

Epilogue..............................111

Bibliography

Preface

A Place Called Hope

Preface

A Place Called Hope

The Matter of Hope is my story of how I lost Hope: Hope, my daughter, and the spiritual concept. Mine is only one story being told while there are thousands of people suffering in silence who have lost HOPE. It is my hope that by telling my story and sharing methods that helped me it may assist you in easing your pain; help you to experience hope in the matters of your life and in the matter of your body to find hope living.

Upon finishing this book it is March of 2015. The moment is all that counts. In this moment in time we are at the threshold of perhaps understanding the deepest parts of ourselves and the Universe. What is matter really made of?

It has been announced that this month in Switzerland the Super Collider will be started up. The Super Collider at CERN will create an experiment to study the tiniest part of the atom. "*On 8 October 2013 the Nobel prize in physics was awarded jointly to François Englert and Peter Higgs "for the theoretical discovery of a mechanism that contributes to our understanding of the origin of mass of subatomic particles, and which recently was confirmed through the discovery of the predicted fundamental particle, by the ATLAS and CMS experiments at CERN's Large Hadron Collider."* This new particle is called the Higgs boson and what they call the God particle. According the CBS News it is called the God particle because "the Higgs boson is what joins everything and gives it matter." And now at CERN they may go further into uniting science and spirituality with their discoveries. Once we understand more fully what the Higgs boson or God particle is, a whole realm of possibilities will open. Hope lives everywhere within matter and within the entire Universe. It symbolizes all that is possible and all that is and, in my own theory, it is called a Place of Hope.

In the Matter of Hope, you will begin to look at just what the titles states, the MATTER of hope. Over the past century, scientists have been questioning the established findings of how our universe, world, and our very beings are put together and how they work. As we all know, beliefs and theories die slowly. In the past the Church was the center of life; Galileo was imprisoned by the church for his theory of the universe. Imprisonment exists within the scientific community today between those who use traditional methods of research and those who go beyond those boundaries. In the last 30 years, there have been huge jumps in understanding of the nature of matter and energy. In many circles in the science community, there are rumblings of proof of what mystics and spiritual men and women have known for centuries. We are made of light, and vibrations are emitted from a FIELD of energy, in the middle of nowhere, right here, right now. We are held together by massive energy and what we perceive and think changes not only our minds, but our bodies, and the very matter around us because of the vibration of our perception. This implies Moses, Jesus, the yogis, and all who can do miracles are really in sync with the FORCE, as they say in Star Wars. These people understand the true nature of the universe. They knew about the Higgs field. "*The Higgs Field is an energy field that exists everywhere in the universe. The field is accompanied by a fundamental particle called the Higgs boson, which the field uses to continuously interact with other particles. As particles pass through the field they are 'given' mass, much as an object passing through treacle (or molasses) will become slower.*" (Wikipedia)

At the memorial for Dr. Martin Luther King, Jr., dedicated this last year, the memorial's concept is based on one of the phrases of his "I Have a Dream" speech:

With this faith, we will be able to hew out of the mountain of despair a stone of hope. With this faith, we will be able to transform the jangling discords of our nation into a beautiful symphony of brotherhood.

It seems in these moments of darkness as a country, family, or in our personal life, we need to hear the words of great men and women speak of Hope. We need to be reminded of this great concept that can lead all of us out into the light once again. And that we do have some control over and responsibility for finding Hope.

And back in 1992, our President-elect spoke at the Democratic Convention and ended his speech with the now famous comment about his home town, "I still believe in a place called Hope." Although that was a campaign speech, I agree: I KNOW there is a place called Hope! Yes, there is Hope: in Arkansas, Kentucky, and Arizona that I know of for sure, but I am not talking about towns. It is a place that is always safe, protected, strong, quiet and inspiring. It is empowering, encouraging, and reassuring. It is not what some say, "A fool's paradise," but actually is a piece of heaven. Maya Angelou tells us *"Everyone must have a place furnished with hope."*

What is Hope? *"Hope is the belief that circumstances in the future will be better. It's not a wish that things will get better, but an actual belief, even when there may be no evidence that anything will change. Hope can encompass a wide variety of beliefs– everything from a high school student hoping for an A in algebra to a cancer patient hoping for a cure."* (Molly Edmonds).

The online dictionary Wikipedia defines hope as the following: "*Hope is the state which promotes the belief in a good outcome related to events and circumstances in one's life. Despair is often regarded as the opposite of hope. Hope is the 'feeling that what is wanted can be had or that events will turn out for the best' or the act of 'look[ing] forward to something with desire and reasonable confidence' or 'feel[ing] that something desired may happen'. Other definitions are 'to cherish a desire with anticipation', 'to desire with expectation of obtainment', or 'to expect with confidence'.*" In the English language the word can be used as either a noun or a verb, although hope as a concept has a similar meaning in either use."

Despair is a dark and desolate place. It is a crippling emotion, and until you have felt it for yourself you cannot ever imagine the pain. *De* is Latin for *without* plus *sperase, to hope,* is the root of despair. *Spei* is to prosper, expand with speed, and as we will see later, comes from the Greek Goddess Spes, Goddess of Hope. Despair is a pit of disappointment, sadness, discouragement, and hopelessness. Hope and despair live in the same neighborhood but are not compatible.

To live with despair you have given up on hope, lost hope, or are without hope. It is to live without joy in tomorrow or in the moment. It is a feeling of numbness and such a suffering place. Whether we have lost a loved one, our home, our health, or a relationship, this place of darkness is very difficult to climb out of for many of us.

Depression is the companion to despair. We now know that depression affects the chemistry in the brain so the cycle of emotion and thought around despair can lead to ongoing daily, lifelong hopelessness. Medicine tells us that this depression starts as a chemical reaction in the brain. But what I believe is it starts with the emotion of despair, and the individual lives in a cycle of despair and negative thoughts, then the body physically changes, not the reverse.

Modern drugs have given many people a new life. And I do think there might be some who already are predisposed to chemical depression who are helped by drugs, but I think most learn it from despair. The drug can help for some time, but the individual never learns to work through the despair and find true hope. The drugs only give them the ability to live a functional life. Once off the drug, some begin to feel the true positive thoughts and emotions and no longer need the drugs. Others go directly back into the spiral of despair and depression. Drugs can lead to addictions if the person isn't already an addict. Addiction is another one-way street to despair, that helpless cycle of loss of control over one's life. Our society leads us to believe that drugs are the way out for all of us, but over the past 20 years, some of us know there are natural ways that have been taught and used for centuries.

I also think that families can teach the members despair, whether it is from loss of members of the family, poverty, or racism. These kinds of families have generations of despair. Over time the negative thoughts and effects that come from depression change the body and person's entire world. Just as negative emotions and thoughts can change matter, so can the positive.

To truly stop this cycle, one needs to go to the place where it began. One must begin to feel all the feelings on the other side of the pit of despair, the anger, fear, sadness, disappointment, and confusion, and to understand that these are only fleeting feelings. With faith and love there is light at the end of the tunnel.

The place of Hope that Dr. King or Presidents Clinton and Maya Angelou are speaking of is a place deeply ingrained in our DNA, in our very matter, as human beings. It is a concept, not an emotion. It is not about wishing. It never leaves; we leave it. It is a stable constant place ever present in the moment. "Faith, Hope, and greatest of these is Love" is what they and I am speaking about. It is a concept that outside of time or space is ever present and can be viewed just by stepping out your door and seeing it in nature.

We find ourselves lost and calling out to hope in despair. When we have a significant loss in our lives, we do not know where we are in time and space. Our thoughts are of sadness and despair; however, our thoughts can change with the snap of the finger. There are "Aha" moments that bring us to places we never thought we could go. As the TV shrink Dr. Phil says, "There is no reality, only perception."

As you practice the shift in perceptions and choices, the thoughts begin the change, and the emotions create transformation in the body and mind. In her book, *The Field, The Quest for the Secret Force of the Universe*, author Lynne McTaggart states, "*Nothing in the universe existed as an actual 'thing' independently of our perception of it. Every minute of every day we were creating our world.*" This statement is based on quantum physics studies postulating that the new science proves that there is a relationship between the observer and what he is observing. In other words, this new discovery changes everything we have come to know about the nature of reality. Dr. Phil, it seems, is totally correct.

My reality, or perception, is there is nothing but hope. Your perception may be there is no more hope. What is our true reality? I would ask what is it that you would like to feel or what would you love for your reality to be? One of despair or a life of ongoing hope day after day, no matter what loss comes your way?

Now is the time to begin.

This is a WORKBOOK. It is an active, not passive, book. You will read sections and then be given exercises to help or to illustrate a point. It is about your emotions, your thoughts, perceptions and more.

As you will see, our thoughts affect our emotions and vice versa. Our spirit can transmute our body, our emotions, and thought. This is how matter can be changed, just by the switching of the mind from negative thoughts and sadness to love and joy.

You are reading this because of some disappointments in your life. You are going through a symbolic drought of the soul. There may have been devastation and oppression of emotions and thoughts. You may feel heaviness in your body and heart. However, the fact that you are reading this material in this moment means you are ready to begin to build your life back from that place of sorrow and despair to a place of hope.

It is the beginning of building your life anew. The cornerstone is Hope. Finding that cornerstone is the goal of this work. We will construct new ways of thinking and feeling with a stronger body and a joyful spirit. You are the developer of your own life. You will self-govern yourself with no need for worldly assistance. You are a student, and your life is the teacher. The conflict and confusion are motivators; they can be the seeds of clarity and harmony. Opposites are part of life. Where there is life, there is death, male and female, and joy and sorrow. They are the same, but from a different perspective.

Decisions are hard to make at times like this, if not totally impossible. You will discover boundaries of the material world; the mind, emotions, and spirit that will help you find your path to Hope. Like the front cover of this book, you have come to a crossroad in your life. You may want to go north or south, maybe east but you cannot see the way. You stand in the center feeling that this point is a nowhere place. You come to learn that it is the beginning place. Once you find the cornerstone, we can build walls that construct a new life.

Things may feel as if they are falling apart. Or you may feel as if you are hanging on by a thread. Think of a nail or tack, a needle at the end of that thread; these are holding and supporting you. These are the people, rituals, and places that give us strength during these times of trials.

> *Hope is the thing with feathers*
> *That perches in the soul,*
> *And sings the tune without the words*
> *And never stops at all.*
>
> (Emily Dickinson)

By using myths and symbolic language, we can tap into places where our left-brained logical minds are confused, and the creative mind is activated to help build a new life of hope. Myths are used to show us that people through the ages have experienced what you are in this moment experiencing in the physical world. You will be able to see yourself in the stories as if someone knows just what your life is like. This is an archetype. It eases the pain and makes sense of the turmoil, knowing that it is a part of all life.

You will see patterns; negative and positive cycles. You will notice there are times to embrace the negative and then time to let it go, no clinging to the past and send in the positive. You will see how negative thoughts lead to disappointment, which makes stagnant emotions and creates illness and disaster after disaster in our world. You will be taking power within yourself to create the kind of patterns that can lead to faith and hope. As with nature the volcano creates molten rock to build new ground; you will learn that through the difficulties in life you can have breakthroughs.

We will learn that the stagnant, frozen state must go, and that we must literally move our bodies, minds, emotions, and spirit. As the cycles tell us, there is a time for everything, but if you are reading this, it is time to change and move to looking for hope. Pretending sometimes is the first step to knowing. Just the movement without thinking what you are doing may be the only thing you can do. Like magic, you begin to believe or do believe because now you are surrounded by new views.

Nature is one of those magical vantage points, and by spending more time in the outdoors you will begin to breathe and feel better. Just a walk in the moonlight lightens your load. You will begin to perceive, or look at, things from a new vantage point: you will move from that crossroads position and turn back to see your experience from a new perception. Our spirit is the engine for this movement. It pulls at our heart.

Synchronicity speaks louder than words. Those are the moments when we find ourselves in that place of wonder while standing in our shoes, in our own bodies and not asleep dreaming, that we know something wonderful is happening. Synchronicities are something mysterious and positive aligning to show us the way of hope.

On this journey to finding new perceptions, you will learn how to form, build, and continue to create a healthy new world of hope for yourself. Through meditation, new thought discipline, exercises in emotional expression, and spiritual quests, you will create a life of hope for yourself. The key to all understanding lies in our DNA. Ultimately, it is all about finding balance in your mind, body, spirit and emotions after having a shock in your life.

I do not subscribe to any organized religion in this body of work, but do center it around spirituality. Spirituality is all inclusive and may or may not include belonging to or practicing a certain religion. Whether you have a belief or not, this book can still speak to you.

President Barack Obama spoke at the dedication for Martin Luther King's Memorial, and I was reminded that he wrote and named his book after this concept hope. In his book the *Audacity of Hope* he writes: "*...a phrase that my pastor, Rev Jeremiah A. Wright Jr., had once used in a sermon—the audacity of hope. That was the best of American spirit, I thought, having the audacity to believe despite all the evidence to the contrary that we could restore a sense of community to a nation torn by conflict; the gall to believe that despite personal setbacks, the loss of a job, or an illness in the family, or a childhood mired in poverty, we had some control, and therefore responsibility, over our own fate.*"

The memorial to Dr King illustrates of what I speak. From the mountain of despair the stone of hope steps forward with King's image. We step forward apart from despair and stand fully clothed in Hope. We are made of atoms. We are made of the same building blocks as the stars. Every part of our DNA is made from that energy. This is the matter of our very being and deep within our DNA are secrets yet to be discovered.

At CERN they are about to smash the atom and find out the nature of matter. I just found out 2 weeks ago that the name of the experiment the actual act of smashing the atom to understand the Higgs boson particle was named; "A Large Ion Collider Experiment: ALICE." And their newsletter is called Alice Matters. I will have to say it did take my breath away. It was another synchronistic message that I was to keep moving forward to make my statement that the Place of Hope is deep inside of our very being in matter.

It was as if spirit were speaking directly to me. Alice matters. We all Matter. It is why we are in the physical; to matter. We matter to each other. We matter to the world. Each of us has a message or job to do while we are alive. We cannot say or do those jobs if we do not have hope. Each person needs to know there is hope no matter what our circumstances.

Everyone must have a place furnished with hope. You are about to not only furnished your place but create your own place of Hope.

You Deserve to Be Happy

The stillness of hope is the expression of a perfect focusing of energy on the task at hand. The stillness of hope is, therefore, the stillness of integrity. Hope integrates. It makes whole.

(Brother David Steindl-Rast)

You deserve to be happy ... remember that.

If you are reading this, you have had some sort of loss or change; if NOT, you have had at some time in your life. Some things to remember are:

- Initially, you may have heightened senses.
- Next, senses feel numb.
- Sense of earthly time is totally off.
- You become aware of things that you have never noticed before.
- Move from apathy to over sensitive, a roller coaster of one or the other.
- The thoughts of "Why did this happen to me?" and, "This is not really happening," the first stage of grief.

The five stages of grief are:
           1) DENIAL
           2) ANGER
           3) BARGAINING
           4) DEPRESSION
           5) ACCEPTANCE

Before you read on, I would like you to answer some of the following questions. This is for you to begin to think about the subject and then to go back after you have read the entire book and re-do these questions.

Does hope have any impact in your life today?

Why should we learn about hope?

What are your expectations or HOPES as you begin this book?

What does hope mean for you as we begin?

The inner world is the world of your requirements and your energies and your structure and your possibilities that meets the outer world. And the outer world is the field of your incarnation. That's where you are. You've got to keep both going. As Novalis said, 'The seat of the soul is there where the inner and outer worlds meet.'

(Joseph Campbell)

Alice Pregnant with Hope

Song for Hope

What started out as any other day...
I wouldn't know I'd never be the same.
Suddenly the lights went out.
I fell so hard. I hit the ground.
Time stopped and I asked why.

I left myself. I couldn't stand the pain.
Resentment filled me...darkened all my day.
I work so hard to make things right.
This can't be all. Who do I fight?
...Silence filled my mind.

I thought about the lessons in my life,
...and reasons for the sadness and the plight.
Where's the sense of fairness here?
Please explain. I want this clear.
A child taken away.
My child's been taken away.

I'm working through this...a bit more every day.
I search for meaning...I find it whenever I pray.

It started out the same as any day.
How could I know I'd never be the same?
Courage, strength and learning how.
It all makes sense...I see that now.
The child came here in faith.
The child He sent my way.

For Hope, I'll see one day.

(Denise Bennett)

Hope is like the sun, which, as we journey towards it, casts the shadow of our burden behind us. Hope sweetens the memory of experiences well loved. It tempers our troubles to our growth and our strength. It befriends us in the dark hours, excites us in bright ones. It lends promise to the future and purpose to the past. It turns discouragement to determination.

(Samuel Smiles)

Introduction

My Story of Hope

It is the winter of your soul.
Time to go into the cave and hibernate
from the rest of the world,
Lick your wounds and forget the daily events.
This is the time to rest,
Allow your body to care for itself.
While you sleep away this harsh cold, dark, lonely winter
Before you sleep hold in your mind,
the vision of the green of spring pushing through the earth.
It will happen; it is the way it works, and the cycles never end,
Winter and Spring,
Despair and Hope.

(Alice Molter-Serrano)

Introduction

My Story of Hope

> "Who are you?" said the Caterpillar.
> This was not an encouraging opening for a conversation.
> Alice replied rather shyly,
> "I—I hardly know Sir, just at the present—
> at least I know who I *was* when I got up this morning,
> but I think I must have been changed several times since then."
>
> (Lewis Carroll)

My name is Alice, and I have always known who "I am", at least, I thought I did. With my baby daughter's death, that part of knowingness died with her. After that I knew nothing. Like the line spoken by Alice in Wonderland, I knew before and during my pregnancy. But the day of her birth I, like Alice in Wonderland, changed many times.

Hope was born on August 26, 1993 and died within moments of her birth. Hope introduced herself to me as my daughter and in a whisper of a moment changed herself into despair. I met them both at the same time. But what I have learned since her birth is, only with looking despair square in the face, can one truly see hope gazing back at you.

I had met up with despair in the past. However, not even the early death of my closest friend and brother was it really despair. Nor did I become introduced to despair with the discovery that the man I loved was in the spiral of alcoholism. In these difficult times, there were moments when I would see the shadow of despair, but never did we look into each other's eyes.

I thought I had always had known hope. After each hardship or sorrow, I felt there was something else to follow, to make "all new again." What I did know as hope turned out to be denial of whom and what I really understood and who I really was.

Hope and despair live in the same dwelling; they are the same but with opposite faces. And I had met both in one instant with my daughter's birth and death.

> In the movie
> *Shawshank Redemption,* Andy says,
> "Hope is a good thing, and no good thing ever dies."

Hope, truly higher hope, never dies. Hope and my daughter were no longer with me. I could not see either of them. But hope is always present even when we can't see it. When our loved ones pass, though we cannot see them in the physical, they are with us in spirit. It is only our perception that they no longer exist. Our loved ones are a part of us, and their energy never dies. And the highest hope for all of us is eternal; it is ironic that it is our greatest losses that lead us to this understanding. My baby had left me as soon as she entered this world, and I thought all my hopes were gone. Despair lead me down a dark path, and I thought I could never return to this world whole, let alone have any hope ever again.

In those moments and days to follow, I felt as if I were Alice in Wonderland. It all felt so unreal, so surreal. The doctors and nurses in the hospital felt it as well. No one in the history of the hospital had given their baby to science. You see, after Hope's birth and her death, my husband and I decided the only way to make sense out of all of it was to give some other family hope. We did decide to give Hope to science, and it is the biggest reason I did not go insane.

Years later, I would learn that my husband felt the opposite way. I shared with him why it made all the difference in the world for me. Hope could at least, with her small body, give another baby a chance. Maybe someone somewhere needed an organ or skin so their baby could live. The scientists could study our daughter to learn more about the disorder to help save other children. We could give other families Hope. If we had not given her to science, I do not think I could have lived through that ordeal. After all, I was alive and that spiritual concept, Hope, needed to live within me and continue to grow. This one single decision turned her passing around from death back to life and hope once again. However, it did not come to me overnight. The journey was just beginning.

"I can't explain *myself*, I'm afraid, sir," said Alice, "because I'm not myself, you see."
"I don't see," said the Caterpillar.
"I'm afraid I can't put it more clearly," Alice replied very politely, "for I can't understand it myself to begin with; and being so many different sizes in a day is very confusing."
"It isn't," said the Caterpillar.
"Well, perhaps you haven't found it so yet," said Alice, "but when you have to turn into a chrysalis—you will some day, you know—and then after that into a butterfly, I should think you'll feel it a little queer, won't you?"
"Not a bit" said the Caterpillar.
"Well, perhaps your feelings may be different," said Alice. "All I know is it would feel very queer to *me*."
"You!" said the Caterpillar contemptuously. "Who are *you*?"
Which brought them back again to the beginning of the conversation.

(Lewis Carroll)

Like Alice in Wonderland, I was afraid, sad, angry, and confused. This was the way my inner dialogue spoke to me. The caterpillar is that never changing subconscious voice that asks questions, one after the other. It is a never-ending loop that leads back to the origin of the questioning of yourself. This is the timeless ever-curious self. This caterpillar will never go through the chrysalis state himself. He is the one that leads the way into the chrysalis state for you. The chrysalis is the state that is not yet adult, but then again, not a larvae. It is a place of protection still inside the cocoon. It is the rebirth of the caterpillar into the butterfly. I continued to ask myself these questions, "Who am I?" and "Where am I?" Following this traumatic event in my life, could I be reborn?

I had lived through it, but it did not seem real. When something of this magnitude happens to us, we struggle to make sense of it. The mundane world cannot answer our questions. It was the language of the poet, the mystic, and the stories of survivors of tragic events that made me feel alive again. There were no words that could express and explain these deep moments, and yet it was necessary for clarity and for healing to do so. For the first time, I had an understanding that these myths and stories were not just for entertainment but were lifeboats for those of us drowning in a storm of trouble. The world of the mystic and myths were and are living entities. These lived and interacted within my own story. There were times when it seemed as if I had become the main character. This is why these stories and myths exist, to explain the unexplainable and to express the vast sea of emotions. We must become the character in the myth and say, "This too has happened to me". My story seemed as if it were a myth, even to me.

The year was 1985 and I had just learned I was pregnant with our first child. We sat in the dark and named our children. My husband and I started talking about the list of names for our baby before the sun had set. As the light in the windows of our Chicago apartment began to dim, we kept talking on into the darkness. It felt right. Turning on the light would have broken our concentration, and besides, for such a sacred moment as giving our offspring her or his signature for life, it called for being in a place of magic and wonder. The light would come on once we had gleaned the names of our children.

Before it was over, at least three hours had gone by. It took forever to name our boy. My husband wanted him to have a strong name. I wanted to use a Hispanic name in keeping with his culture, but he wanted something neutral; after all, the last name gave him the Puerto Rican identity. It must have taken two hours and 45 minutes to come up with Stephen. But when it came to a girl's name, it just presented itself with no struggle.

I had been working in an inner city school for the past eight years with kids that they liked to label "at risk." It was a high school, and as far as I was concerned, all teens are at risk. One day I was walking down the hall with a Special Education teacher who was also a friend of mine. (I don't remember what had just happened, but something always happened as you walked those halls.) She turned to me and said, "Alice, do you know what you do in this school?" I thought for a moment and wasn't sure just what she was getting at. "What do you mean?" was my reply. She continued, "You give everyone Hope; you walk through the halls each day, and no matter what happens or who it is, you never give up, and you spread hope to everyone."

I was very surprised. I had never thought of myself in that light. I thanked her for the wonderful compliment and then we went on to talk about the topic of hope. I guess my friend was the messenger from above, for this is where the entire journey began. It really woke me up. And I thank my dear friend from the bottom of my heart, for she has given me a name for the concept I had been living all my life. I would ponder her words and observe my own behavior just to understand what she saw in me.

So when it came time to naming our daughter, my husband reminded me of this, the quality of HOPE. He said what an honor for our baby girl to be named after the quality that you had carried with you each and every day. There would be no discussion; her name was Hope. However, Hope was not here yet. Stephen arrived on July 16th, 1986, with eyes wide open. It would be seven years before Hope entered our lives, and much was to happen before and after her arrival.

I had a desire to write about women's issues, and I had been doing research into the most ancient of cultures. I wasn't yet sure of where I was going with the work. I only knew I had a desire to make sense of a dream I had had in 1992 about myself and a group of women. Upon waking from this dream, it had affected me like none other. It was through this research and writing that I was beginning to find answers. Then, one day months after beginning this project, I became pregnant with Hope. Seven months later, we were to find out, only hours before her birth, that she possessed a genetic defect called Trisomy Thirteen. This defect is a chromosomal imbalance; there are three copies of the 13th chromosome instead of two.

Many tribes do not name their children until after they are born. The tradition is based on the fact that a person should be a reflection of his or her personality. They should not be labeled until those who raise and love them, see who they start to become. Then he or she is named. In the movie

Dances With Wolves the natives found the little white girl and they waited until she showed her characteristics. They also gave the soldier a new name when they saw him playing with the wolf that visited him at his outpost. Dances with Wolves became his name. A significant event or feature gives the person his or her name.

In the Bible, Eve means begetter of life, and Adam comes from the word meaning earth. You find many stories of how the people changed their names. Sarai becomes Sarah, and Abram becomes Abraham. H is the fifth letter of the Hebrew alphabet, and even though it is the fifth, it is considered very sacred. When Abraham and Sarah went to Israel, they added the H to let God know how much they were committed to him. Jacob changes his name totally and called himself Israel. Our parents, tribes or families give us names, but as we get to know ourselves and the world gets to know us, like Jacob, we may feel as if we are someone new.

Rabbi David Wolpe in his book *Making Loss Matter* says, "*When the world forces us to ask who we are, why we want to live, who we want to be, we are confronted by our names.*" He goes on to say, "*Every name is a possibility and a limitation.*" Rabbi Wolpe suggests that it may not be our name that is who we are but that the fact that we have faith in ourselves and our mission in life despite our name. What is our mission in life?

I have thought, who are we? Why do we want to live? Who do we want to be? Does your name fit those questions? I was given a little card for my birthday during my twenties, and on it is the meaning of Alice. It says the Irish Gaelic meaning is "Truthful one, Holy one." Wow, as I read it I was really in doubt that I could live up to it. As the Rabbi Wolpe states, we have a mission, and it may not be in the name we were given. Giving hope had become my mission in life. Naming my daughter after that mission was a risky thing. "Every name is a possibility and a limitation." When hope dies, what happens to the mission?

In our case, my husband only wanted a name for our firstborn boy that was strong. He said it could be nothing that would be made a sing song teasing tool on the playground. But Hope was somehow to be named after me, her mom, and my qualities. After all she would be the chip off the old block, or maybe, a flicker from my own flaming heart. It was almost as if I should have changed my name to Hope as Jacob had taken on the name of Israel. But instead, we desired to physically produce this concept in a baby girl. She was named and thought of eight years before she became a physical reality.

Quantum Physics is now finding out that what we thought was real in our physical world is much different than we thought. Newton was not entirely correct. It tells us that we quite literally can create events and change things by just a thought. That the myths and fairytales of old could ring true. That what we desire can come true. So could it be that my desire to share hope with the world and the wish for a daughter, placed out into the universe eight years earlier had been so strong that my husband and I created her? The joy I felt was unbelievable; I truly believed I was living a dream until she was born and died moments later.

Everything is energy, and that's all there is to it. Match the frequency of the reality you want and you cannot help but get that reality. It can be no other way. This is not philosophy. This is physics.

(Darryl Anka)

When I lost her soul and her little body, the matter of Hope, meaning the physical body of Hope, it led to me into the pit of despair. In giving her body to science, it was the only way I could believe in hope. By the giving of her body, another family may have had a chance for their child so other mothers and fathers would not have to carry this sorrow.

The fact that this matter of Hope, our daughter, gave tangible hope to others was a way of alchemy. That from "something in matter" changed from one thing to another had miraculous power in the spiritual sense. From our loss and despair, we could make what we had wanted into something bigger than our original desire. From our loss, our desire for a daughter, based on the principle of hope and named upon this same principle, could affect and give a greater hope to many more people. But how could we live without our dear sweet daughter in the flesh? Could it be possible for us to ever get to a place where we could understand that our loss became hope for others in our despair?

What does Hope mean in our lives? Why do some know her and others don't? Ultimately, Faith and Love must be the constant companions of this beauty named Hope. On a personal level, I would live in innocence with hope in my heart and would discover who she was, would lose sight of her time after time, only to have her return, live in my heart and become stronger than before.

And so it is with *THE MATTER OF HOPE;* with this writing, I wish to share my experience and truth about hope with all who care to listen. To continue to make sense of this story of mine by giving it away and reaching out to others who have loved and lost, live but feel death, or lack desire to move forward in life. To become an alchemist of HOPE for them, is *my* hope.

Alice in Wonderland was a story that was with me all my life because of my name but when my story turned to the dark side it meant even more to me. These stories in our lives are important as metaphors. Write about what story symbolizes your life. Explain why and how.

How would you finish these sentences?

All my life I hoped for_____

I lost hope when_____

I found hope after_____

In the midst of our struggle to find out who we are, there are infinite possibilities for beauty, and hope, and wonder, and love.

(Mandy Hale)

When the heart is enlivened again, it feels like the sun coming out after a week of rainy days. There is hope in the heart that chases the clouds away. Hope is a higher heart frequency and as you begin to reconnect with your heart, hope is waiting to show you new possibilities and arrest the downward spiral of grief and loneliness.

It becomes a matter of how soon you want the sun to shine.

Listening to the still, small voice in your heart will make hope into a reality.

(Sara Paddison)

Part I

Our Emotional Body

The Heart of the Matter

Give sorrow words. The grief that does not speak whispers the o'er fraught heart and bids it break.

(William Shakespeare)

The fastest way to freedom is to feel your feelings.

(Gita Bellin)

There I was ready to make dinner for my family. I was back to my life after losing my baby. I thought I was fine and life goes on, but there I stood with the refrigerator door wide open. It was full of food and the decision of what to cook was so overwhelming I just stood there, frozen, unable to think. The emotions yet unfelt stopped me in my tracks.

We hear all the time the best way to deal with something or someone difficult is to "come from the heart." I like that idea, but it is easier said than done. What does it mean to come from the heart? First, I think it means to lead with your emotions. It means to not think about the situation so much. I personally think, in the heart, also lies our intuition. So could it be a combination of emotion and intuition, this heart connection?

"Coming from the heart" or "leading with the heart" means to listen to our emotions and how the situation makes us feel. Feelings are not emotions; it took me a long time to understand this one. Feelings are the physical manifestation of an emotion. So let us say someone says a wonderful thing to you like, "You have made my life more meaningful by your being here with me." You hear it and there is an instant emotional response, right brain stuff. Then you feel the feeling of love, joy, or whatever feeling it may evoke. What we are talking about is the right side of our brain. But this is only to a certain extent. Haven't you had an experience where someone made a statement, either negative or positive, and you felt it go right to your heart? There is a literal pain in your heart. Or when there is love or a positive emotion the heart feels full. Our bodies respond accordingly to the emotion evoked. This is why we call it *Coming* from the Heart. It physically feels that way. And who knows, maybe the physical heart does have a part in it. This is the matter of the heart.

The right brain holds a wealth of operations from creativity to sense of space and time. It is a mysterious area, and it can do unpredictable and incredible things. Researchers are not totally sure how the brain functions with emotions. They do know that when a person loses the left side of the brain, he may lose speech, but the gracious, flexible right brain will regroup and teach the person to speak again.

The most unproductive, empty, fruitless fellow in the world is the man with a barren heart. Happiness can never reach him, for nothing good and lasting can lodge in his heart. It is solid as a billiard ball. Contrast this man with his barren heart with the human that plays the game of life fairly and honestly and is willing to make others happy by his own sacrifices.

(F. D. Van Amburgh)

But now research is telling us what many of us have always thought, the heart has its own brain. From the Institute of HeartMath comes great knowledge concerning our hearts. They tell us that the heart is a sensory organ and constantly sends the brain signals. It enables us to learn, remember, and is involved in how we perceive thing by how we feel about them. The heart and brain work in tandem with each other.

They propose that the heart has a field that acts as a carrier for information to the entire body that helps to synchronize how it works. A person's emotional state is communicated throughout the entire body through the heart. Negative emotions, such as anger, frustration, are associated with disorder in the heart's rhythms. But positive emotions like appreciation, and compassion lets the heart run smoothly and in order with the rest of the body.

HeartMath says:

…deepened awareness and consciousness results…from the body's internal physiological, emotions, and metal processes, and also of the deeper, latent orders enfolded into energy fields that surround us. This is the basis of self-awareness, social sensitivity, creativity, intuition, spiritual insight, and understanding of ourselves and all that we are connected to. It is through the intentional generation of coherence in both heart and social fields that a critical shift to the next level of planetary consciousness can occur—one that brings us into harmony with the movement of the whole.

From Mindful Muscle, the Heart has its Own "Brain" and Consciousness:

The heart generates the body's most powerful and most extensive rhythmic electromagnetic field. Compared to the electromagnetic field produced by the brain, the electrical component of the heart's field is about 60 times greater in amplitude, and permeates every cell in the body.

So the Matter of our Heart has everything to do with what we think, perceive and know. How we feel influences everything. Do we even know what we are feeling most of the time? In this society so much has been placed on the mental level and the brain that the heart, this most important organ and generator of emotion, gets left out. It seems only when experiences like loss, betrayal, compassion, and deep love happen are we aware of how powerful the heart is to us.

Symbolism is a good way to deal with understanding our feelings. The moon has forever been a symbol for emotions.

The closest celestial body to the earth, the moon, has a force of gravity powerful enough to cause the earth to bulge slightly where the moon passes over. This pull is most noticeable in the oceans, causing high tides. The fluid aspect of all the creatures of Earth and her oceans are affected by changes in the light and the pull of the moon. The moon also rules the watery realms of the consciousness, perception, and emotions.

(We'Moon)

Is it any wonder that for eons we have called the moon a symbol for our emotions? There are phases in our lives, and our emotions reflect those phases. The full moon, waning, waxing, new moon, crescent moon, and quarter moons are all phases. When gardening or farming, the Farmers' Almanac explains the best time to work with your crops. There are times to plant, the dark of the moon; and there are times to have seed germinate, the new moon. There is a rhythm and ebb and flow. There is birth, growth, fullness, diminishment, and disappearance, and then rebirth and growth again. So it is with our lives.

Our heart keeps the body alive with its never ending rhythm. The beating of our heart is a cycle like the seasons. Intense love can make it speed up or fear can make it jump a beat. The depth of the heart and what that means to us has yet to be revealed by the mind. Only in the heart can we understand.

When we become stuck in phases because of pain, we cannot move emotionally or in any way. As with the full moon, Luna, lunacy may happen in our lives when we do not express our deepest feelings. We are in denial about how painful something has been, and we place our emotions on hold or pretend everything is ok. This cannot last for long. Either the unexpressed emotion makes us ill, or we emotionally break.

This is the matter of the heart.

The same is true with expressed positive emotions. When we feel joy or love, it heals us physically. Many doctors have seen this happen over and over again. Studies have shown when we laugh, there are chemicals in the brain, which are released that make the body feel in balance and healthy.

This is the matter of the heart.

When we feel hopeless and in despair, we are not sure if this is true. If we become stuck, we feel as if the pain and depression will never leave.

Having awareness of what we are feeling and naming it is important.
Sometimes the pain is so vast that we can't see or feel what is wrong. We feel numb. This is a protection from the hurt. As I stated before, at some point it is released or forced out in some way.

Beginning to become aware of your emotions is the start.

How are you feeling at this moment? How does your body feel? What does your body language tell you?

Write this all down now.

Now think of the following emotions, and write your physical response, body language, and what action, if any, you usually take:

Anger:

Joy:

Excitement:

Sorrow:

Becoming aware of your emotions and how you react can lead to positive reaction and thoughts.

Most of us don't think about our emotions; we just feel or don't feel them. If you have had a loss, it feels as if a part of you is gone or dead. There is an emotional wound. As with wounds on the body, if they are not taken care of they will become infected and will make you ill.

Unexpressed emotion is like a stagnant pool of water. It sits and festers; it becomes murky and unclear. When emotions are expressed in the moment, the flow of your life moves forward. However, like a stagnant pool, if we sit in our emotions without expression in some way, all kinds of strange actions appear. Illness, outbursts at odd times, meanness, loneliness and more, emerge.

We can be here now when we accept instantly our moment by moment emotional experience.
(Gita Bellin)

When the shock of our loss is over, we can once again be able to feel. It is okay to feel, in fact, it is a must. Our emotions are our barometer, our protector, and ultimately, the way to our love of life.

1. Finding a safe place and/or person to express feelings to is very important.
2. I found writing was about the only action I could take at first.
3. Reading subjects that have to do with what you are experiencing or doing, something fun or, is helpful.
4. Then reaching out to others who love you is part of the process.
5. Later, attending support groups eases the pain.

6. Reaching out to others who have had the same experiences is the next step. When I was able, I wanted to reach out to strangers who had gone through similar experiences. This step was not one of "my asking for help", but my helping others. This last step is what really moved my emotions and opened my heart. This experience is the matter of the heart. Rebirth and creating new ideas and relationships from our deep emotional pain is a coming out of that emotional loneliness. I must add, it was the most difficult thing I did. And it was THE thing that moved me back into the world in a positive way.
7. You may not feel like it right now, but laughter is such good medicine. Watch a favorite funny movie or talk to one of your fun friends and tell them "make me laugh"!
8. Children are a great release and bring joy. However, as in my case, I had to wait for some time to be around other people's children; my son was a joy and the reason I went on!

MOVE!

Physical activity is a must.
- Walking either with someone or alone can help.
- Yoga or gentle exercise works, too. You can exercise at home at first, follow tapes, or invite a friend to join you.
- Put on some music and dance—alone!
- If you have physical limitations, take a drive, or ask a friend to go on a drive. Just by leaving the places you know can pry you loose.

These moments of emotions flowing are not linear in nature; they come and go. There are no judgments with feelings. They are emotions, and how you react is totally unique to you and only you.

Be gentle with yourself.
- Take baths when stressed, and relax your tight muscles.
- Ask for touch from loved ones—hugs or long periods of holding.
- Sit in the sunshine, or in the case of emotions, I liked to sit in the moonlight. Being in the dark and quiet with the moon on my face felt as if the moon was drawing out the sadness and fear. It was a gentle touch.
- Be with close friends to do nothing, just watch TV, or have dinner together.

Like the moon, natural beauty eases the pain.
- Beauty can move us to tears and great joy. This includes great pieces of art and music.
- Theater and movies are also a way to remain silent but move our emotions.
- A long walk in the woods or listening to a favorite piece of music is inspiring.
- Animals are great. They do not talk back. If you have a pet, sit quiet with this little creature and just BE! If you don't have one, get a pet.

All of these are ways to move forward in a smooth and gentle way. You will be looking at other ways to deal with your emotions and ways to turn negative responses into positive thoughts.

I recently read a piece by Ram Dass. He says: In allowing ourselves to grieve, we learn that the process is not cut and dried. It's more like a spiral that brings us to a place of release, abates for a time, and then continues on a deeper level. Often, when grieving, we think that it's over, only to find ourselves swept away by another wave of intense feeling. For this reason, it's important to be patient with the process, and not be in a hurry to put our grief behind us.

Be gentle and take your time.

Transformation does not occur from changes in the world outside us; we create the miracle ... from within.
(Jacquelyn Small)

Fear

**You gain strength, courage & confidence every experience
in which you really stop to look fear
in the face. You must do the thing which you think
you cannot do.**

(Anna Eleanor Roosevelt)

Fear is a funny thing when it comes to loss. Whether it is a loss of a marriage, career, or loved one dying, in most cases fear preceded the loss. You are hanging on to hope during these times. Hope that this loss is not going to happen. You become used to the fear. When the moment of truth happens we blame hope, not the fear. We tell ourselves hope was a lie, false hope, when all along we did not really look at our fears realistically. We do not want to face the facts.

Letting go of fear takes time and practice. When we learn to dance or learn a new language we have to do it over and over again. We make mistakes and then study and do it again. We *try* different ways to retain what we learn and ways to discard what does not work. It is the same with learning to live without fear. As with anxiety, we must first label the fear. If we do not know what we are afraid of we live in the darkness of paralyzing terror, even afraid to look the *very* thing in the face. Seeing the face of our fear sheds light in the darkness. Beyond the anxiety of everyday life what are you afraid to face?

I must not fear. Fear is the mind-killer. Fear is the little-death that bring total obliteration. I will face my fear. I will permit it to pass over me & through me. And when it has gone past I will turn the inner eye to see its path. Where the fear has gone there will be nothing. Only I will remain.

(Frank Herbert)

I was afraid to face other people. I stayed home for months. I finally had enough courage to pick up my son from school and even went and waited for him at a picnic table in the playground. I was terrified that I would have to speak to someone. And then it happened; a woman I knew and who worked at the school saw me from across the playground. She stopped and I saw the fear on her face. She was as afraid as I was. I could see her making a decision to keep walking or to acknowledge me. She waved and then she started walking toward me. Now I was terrified. How would I get through this conversation? She hugged me and told me the traditional "I am so sorry." But here was the funny part: she was more afraid and upset about it all than I was. I sat there listening to her talk about how she had felt about our experience of losing our baby. About how she felt so much for our son and how she was looking out for him at school. Then she began to cry. I found myself comforting her. This was not what I expected. My fear of meeting others in public kept me locked up inside for months when all along I had a misconception of what others felt and how it would be. I learned that when someone losing a child, a baby; it touches something deep in them. Their own fears of such an event and losing their loved ones could happen to them.

Letting go of grief takes COURAGE. When you have decided that it is okay to be happy again and stop the grieving or the grieving is finished, you become brave about living again. The fear of leaving the loved one or life you once knew behind seems so impossible. Living life takes courage.

Practice looking at fear in the face over and over again until you become one with the fear. Let the fear become your friend. Then when you have done that over and over again you can leave it and turn to look into the light of faith and trust.

When we have had loss there is a lot of change. When change is sudden or a major disruption to your life it is very scary. What do I do now? How am I going to get through this? Even if you have people around to support , deep inside the fear grasps you in your silence.

Faith and trust replaces the face of your fear. Then we can hope.

Try this exercise:

Day 1. (There will be 5 days to this exercise.)

This first part of the exercise is a visualization: Close your eyes and see yourself looking in a mirror. Now see yourself looking in the mirror over your shoulder to the back of you. or using an imaginary hand mirror to reveal what is off to the left of you or behind you, as if the fear is lurking there. Now look over your shoulder at the fears. What is your fear? If you fear speaking in public see yourself in front of an audience or if you fear being alone see yourself alone. Look at it, do not turn away. Spend a few moments doing this.

Now look back at the mirror and see yourself directly in front of you. Now switch again to looking behind you, at the fear. Now back at yourself. Spend several moments looking at only your image.

Open your eyes.

Next you will actually be doing this exercise in a real mirror. Go to the bathroom or bedroom and look in a real mirror at your reflection. Know that this is you! Look over your shoulder, in the mirror at your fear. Now look back at your reflection!

Fears are masks we make to keep us from truth and hope.

You are real. Your fears are only illusions of your mind. You are here NOW! Look behind you in the mirror and there is nothing there.

Character isn't inherited. One builds it daily by the way one thinks & acts, thought by thought, action by action. If one lets fear or hate or anger take possession of the mind, they become self-forged chains.
(Helen Ganesha Douglas)

Each day remember your fears are only illusions in your mind. Truth is faith, love, trust and HOPE.

Day 2. Check your fear! Do day 1 visualization of looking at your fear. Now look at yourself. Today when you look at yourself say the following:

I am full of grace.
I am real and here now.
I can change the way I feel and think.
I am in control of my fears.

I am the focus of my life.

Repeat these while looking at yourself and then as you go about your day. You are more than the sum of all your fears. Fears are only "your negative thoughts" and you can change your thoughts in the flash of a second.

Day 3. Today look at your fear again, look at it in the face. Know it again. Now see yourself in the mirror, who do you like to look at more, your fear or your own reflection? Hopefully, it is YOU!

Now repeat the statements from yesterday. Today we are going to look at trust.

> "Come to the edge," he said.
> "We can't, we're afraid!" they responded.
> "Come to the edge," he said.
> "We can't, We will fall!" they responded.
> "Come to the edge," he said.
> And so they came.
> And he pushed them.
> And they flew."
>
> (Guillaume Apollinaire)

What emotional response does this quote bring up in you?
If this is you…who or what do you trust to push you?
What or who is it? Name it and write it down.

Now look at yourself again and repeat who or what you trust out loud.

This is the time to take the jump, the fear you selected; what stops you when you are living in this fear? (Example: Fear of speaking in front of people would result in not taking jobs that have to do with being in front of others, and as result you may not get as much income or responsibility because of this decision. This stops you from progressing.)

How can your trust help you with your fear? Write it here.

Consult not your fears but your hopes & your dreams. Think not about your frustrations, but about your unfulfilled potential. Concern yourself not with what you tried & failed in, but with what it is still possible for you to do.
(Pope John XXIII)

Now look at yourself and say out loud:
I trust (whatever it is) to remove all of this fear.
I am the only thing that will remain.
I can and will go on without this fear in my life.
I have faith that I will live with hope once again.

I steer my bark with hope in the head, leaving fear astern. My hopes indeed sometimes fail, but not oftener than the foreboding of the gloomy.
(Thomas Jefferson)

Day 4. Today: Look at yourself and say several times:

I have fear but trust my hopes more than my fears!

From now on never ignore your fears or you will live in them unaware of them. You go on no matter what and face the fear until it dissolves. Then have the courage to move forward.

Day 5. Remember that old saying, "take the tiger by the tail"? Well, now that is what we need to do each day of our lives.

After all, when we do grab his/her tail, we turn to see there is no tiger, only that the tiger has gone into you and you greet the day with fierce optimism. The lie is fear, it is only an illusion that keeps us from our truth!

I once heard it said, if you are afraid of ghosts or evil spirits just laugh, they hate that and they will leave you alone. Whether you believe in ghosts or not, the real ghosts are our fears, and if we keep a healthy sense of humor in our pocket as we look at our fears life will be full of more joy and hope!

All of us are born with a set of instinctive fears-of falling, of the dark, of lobsters, of falling on lobsters in the dark or speaking before a Rotary Club & of the words "Some Assembly Required."

(Dave Barry)

Place this on your mirror:

I am full of grace.
I am real and here now.
I can change the way I feel and think.
I am in control of my fears.
I am the focus of my life.

The Matter of Anger

Anybody can become angry-that is easy; but to be angry with the right person, and to the right degree, and at the right time, and for the right purpose, and in the right way—that is not within everybody's power and it is not easy.

(Aristotle)

Anger in matter is a very disturbing thing. It creates disease, violence of all shapes and forms, and tears at the very fabric of our society. However, it has its purpose and can protect and support us if noted and dealt with positively. No emotion is bad, it is how we use and view the emotion that makes the difference.

Anger arises from change, confusion or dissatisfaction. In loss there is certainly all of these. So with these three looming, it is only logical that after we have lost a part of us that we react with anger. Grief has begun and anger is one of the stages of the process of grief. We feel confused at the change in our life and are dissatisfied. First there is denial. We are confused because this could not have happened to ME. It happens to others but not me. Then there is anger when we realize that it has happened to us, whether it is a divorce or a death, it is out in the open and we know it is real.

When we become angry with ourselves we must be aware not to turn it inward. The release of anger is very important and a normal part of the process. In fact, a lack of anger is a barrier to growth.

Most often the result of pent up frustrations, repressed, anger can turn inward in destructive, paralyzing ways. It can prevent us from dealing positively with problems or relating lovingly to others, and can also lead to serious health disorders.

(Harper's Bazaar)

It is difficult to find a quote that is positive about anger. This emotion is frightening to us. It seems so violent and religion has taught us to suppress this emotion because it is so negative. No emotion is negative; it is how we deal with an emotion that leads to negative results. Every emotion has a purpose or it would not exist. I have said before it is up to us to be aware of what we are feeling and become responsible for expressing it in a productive way. In the West we are not taught to deal with our feelings. But here is the problem, it takes skill and maturity to understand how to deal with our feelings as they arise. Anger is normal and needs to be a part of our lives and has to be transmuted when dealing with loss.

The ancient Greeks spoke of anger as a much needed part of a spiritual person. Jacob Needleman, a philosopher and author, says anger is a difficult one to translate from this Greek perspective. It comes from the word *thumos* and it relates to spiritedness, like a spirited horse.

It also describes a part of us that loves victory, struggle and combat. Using what the Greeks considered *nous*, or the higher part of us, anger can be a powerful tool. Armed with our higher self anger can improve life both inside of ourselves as well as the world.

There are theories about depression being anger turned inward. The experts have never been sure on how this works. Some say they are totally different emotions that have nothing to do with the other.

I do know that when we are faced with a difficult life situation such as loss some of us understand that our anger is natural and use it to change our situation. Others of us feel powerless, helpless, and hopeless. Maybe we have learned from society that anger is negative and think that expressing it would only hurt us more.

It is true that when we look at the roots of anger caused by loss it comes from overwhelming sadness and hurt. This is when it transforms into to anger. The anger could be called a kind of mask to protect us from our deepest hurts, until we are ready to feel them or feel them little bits at a time. Angry outbursts can be dangerous if not held and channeled. Lightening is wild electrical energy and can destroy. But a light bulb can light my house. So it is with anger.

So how do we get through this?

> *Emotions follow thought, and thought, fueled by emotion (energy), manifests in the physical world.*
> (Jacquelyn Small)

How we think, positive or negative, creates how we feel. We should not discount emotions or not feel them. but when we are feeling stuck we need to find a way out of this position. Let anger motivate you. As the philosopher Needleman states we need to use what the Greeks called a higher part of ourselves, or better or higher self. Anger is an energy and like any other kind of energy it can be used to transform.

Think of a loss and how you expressed or did not express your anger: explosion, repression or directed toward growth. Write it down.

Do you become angry often or not at all?

This week become aware of your anger. When it comes up feel the fiery nature and do not be afraid or explode. Hold on to it; look at it and feel it. Think about how strong and powerful the anger is. Such energy has a power to change situations and experiences.

Let this power change your perceptions. As you are still feeling the anger, hold it and think of how this power may change things for you. Let it motivate you to do something positive with it. Keep the power of the anger in you belly but keep your mind clear and cool. Through your heart comes the true passion then the heart tells the mind what to do in a calm and clear manner.

Create and take some action based on the energy of the anger but not in anger.

Example: My son tells me he lost my father's ring. My son wore the ring without my knowledge. My father had passed away and it was one last thing I had left to remember him. I become very upset and angry. I wait and keep my mouth shut until I feel the anger. I hold on to it and think of what I really want to say to him. I do not blurt out as I first feel the anger.

Know what anger feels like in your body. Where do you react? Do you feel it in your stomach, your jaw or neck? The body will tell you first. Observe the physical and then acknowledge the anger. Feel the energy of the anger but hold it in the place in your body. Feel it without taking action. Remember, this all happens in the flash of a half second but it does work.

Then think! What is going on? Why am I angry? What do I want to say? I need to say something that will express this anger.

Then use your thoughts and words to express the energy behind the feeling without putting the anger onto the other person or thing.

Many times if a loved one has left us we wish we could speak to them about how we feel about their leaving us. We can do this.

Find a isolated and quiet place and speak to them. No one is actually there but the fact that you are directing the anger at the missing person is the place it needs to go. Maybe put a chair in the middle of the room or imagine they are sitting in front of you on the ground. This can give you focus. Let the anger roll.

Or write a letter to the loved one but don't send it. Let all the anger out on paper. Do not keep the letter throw it out, rip it up or burn it. This tossing away gives you a release of the anger. This is not silly or foolish. It can clear the air and makes room for you to express your sadness and hurt.

> *The principal use of prudence, of self control, is that it teaches us to be masters of our passions, and to so control and guide them that the evils which they cause are quite bearable, and that we even derive joy from them all.*
>
> (Descartes)

I express to my son that I am very angry with him, without name calling, or yelling. I stated I am angry because he is careless and it hurts because that was one last thing of my father's and now it is gone. As I express it to him in a less passionate, aggressive, and threatening manner he is able to take responsibility for his own action and is able to express his remorse without fear of my wrath.

We, together, then talk about how he can make it up to me. Still feeling the anger, but keeping my thoughts open and calm, I state that he needs to trace his steps. I tell him the story of the ring and why it meant so much to me. This diffuses the anger and I feel more sadness than anger. He comments about the story and tells me how sorry he is and will try again to find the ring. If he cannot find it, he says he would like to buy me a ring to replace it. It would be from him and then I can remember both him and my father as I wear it. This makes me cry with joy.

It could have turned into a yelling match with both my son and I separating. I could have blamed him and done nothing but tell him how irresponsible he was. We may never have talked of it again and I could held it over his head for weeks or even years, using the anger to make him suffer. And on top of it I held in the hurt and sadness to nurse the anger only keeping it alive. It could have put a wedge between us. That is how anger from one loss can create another loss. Instead the **power** of the anger pushed me through it only to make us even closer.

Once again, our thoughts can help us filter the anger. If we find ourselves isolated from friends and family after a loss, the same thoughts of the past or distorted thoughts roll through our heads. Being with others who love us and that bring positive attitudes into our minds helps all of our thoughts. We tend to have low self esteem during troubled times and this brings in negative thoughts and also makes us angry.

It is easier said than done when the pain washes over us. Remember, be good to yourself. Showing your anger is fine and needed. It is better for you to express than repress, despite popular opinion. To have those flashes once in awhile is acceptable but next time try observing what you are feeling before you act.

And, by the way, my son found my father's ring.

Humor

The seed is hope; the flower is joy.

(Unknown)

It takes courage to live—courage and strength and hope and humor. And courage and strength and hope and humor have to be bought and paid for with pain and work and prayers and tears.

(Jerome P. Fleishman)

Living in the moment can bring spontaneous joy. Between my cat and my son, who was seven, these times were often. One day our cat caught a bird. Living in the southwest we would leave our kitchen door open so all in the house could come and go with ease. So on this day, Quasar, our cat, brought the bird in the house. I was unaware of this fact. He took it into the bathroom to put it in the bathtub to chase and play with it. My son came running out of his room yelling "There is a bird in the house, there is a bird in the house." He jumped on the couch and began jumping up and down saying the phrase "There's a bird in the house." As I entered the room the bird came flying out of the bathroom with the cat in pursuit. It flew right for my son who was jumping up and down and almost hit him in the head. He ducked and the bird turned and flew out the open door. Grief could not live in that moment, it broke it all apart.

Laughter is healing. To laugh we must feel joy. As the quote so appropriately says, when we are in a hopeful state we feel joy. From joy comes humor, which comes as such a safety rope to our sanity. It gives us strength. When we can perceive our situation from another view, as an absurdity or a place of detachment, it can add levity to the situation.

When it comes to loss and change, humor seems to be out of place. But when we take a look at our tragedy or change in our life and stand back from it, we may be able to see joy in it all. How can this be you say? For example, if you believe in an afterlife and you have a loved one who passes, you feel your pain of the loss. However, when we look at the spirit of our loved one and truly believe he/she is in another world, a better, freer world, you must feel joy for them. There are cultures that celebrate at a funeral; it is a party, not a somber affair, but full of laughter and joy. Funny stories are told about the loved one and the party is held for them.

Good humor makes all things tolerable.

(Henry Ward Beecher)

What about change such as divorce or loss of a job? At these times we may become sarcastic. Satirical humor is a form of angry humor; it means the tearing of the flesh, so it is not of joy but of pain. However, it is a place to begin. At least anger moves out the sorrow and can lead us to feelings of happiness. While we may be laughing in sarcasm, we might be crying inside. At some point the laughter may turn into the joy of letting go of this relationship or job that, in retrospect, was not good for us.

Taking the time to relax and watch movies like those of the Marx Brothers can bring happiness that is outside of your reality. Harpo is one who is gentle and silent, and this kind of humor can lighten your heart. Or Groucho, with his biting comments that, with the silliness of his mannerisms, may coincide with the way you may be feeling. Either way, it will give some relief. Or maybe you like something more satirical like *National Lampoon's Vacation* with Chevy Chase and Imogene Coca. Other great comedians can give respite to a heavy heart. Allow yourself to find time to find some lightheartedness in the gloom. It may lighten the load.

Humor is a prelude to faith and laughter is the beginning of prayer.
(Reinhold Niebuhr)

So many of the humorous quotes I looked at had trust, faith, hope and laughter, all linked together. If we do not have some way of releasing the pressure, tears or laughter, the pain will fester. Both tears or laughter cleanse us and heal us in times of pain. Laughter quickens the heart and heals our body.

In the book *There Is a Rainbow behind Every Dark Cloud*, Jerry Jamplosky writes *"You can learn to control your mind and decide to be happy 'inside' with a smiling heart, in spite of what happens to you on the 'outside'."*

Remember, no matter what, you deserve and are meant to be happy!

Emotional Time and Space

In a dark time, the eye begins to see.

(Theodore Roethke)

Our emotions and emotional memory affect how we perceive time. When there is trauma in our lives, all time stops. The fellow down the street goes to work, comes home to his family, goes to the movies and has his daily routine; he has no trauma or drastic change in his life. How he perceives time is different from our traumatic life. His time goes on as usual and in some cases, goes by fast, while ours has come to a standstill.

Grief and deep emotion take on a kind of second by second, intense, almost spatial world of its own. Those outside of the event or circumstances are not able to go to this time or place. This is why myths and symbols ring true during these otherworldly occurrences in our lives. These stand the "test of time" and mean the same and feel the same because they are in that place of timelessness. They are touchstones for those of us who have transcended the perceived worldly concepts of time and space. However, once you have experienced a milestone of this magnitude, you will be able to go to or help others when they themselves have arrived there. Even the word's "touchstone" and "milestone" give us a way of measuring how huge this event has become. It needs a special tracking in time and space concepts. It reminds me of the games all of us have played as children, tag or hide and seek. The one safe place is "home base"; here we are safe from harm or the person who is "it". We can stand and watch while we are standing in a place where we can feel secure and unchanged by the threat of "it". The game looks totally different from that position. In real adult life, using these markers, milestones and touchstones, we then measure our lives from that point on. They are our "home", a kind of secure place to view, rest and become slow or at a standstill while the world goes by.

Here is where the emotional memory affects our concept of where we are and what time it is in our minds and hearts. Back to our neighbor down the road: his life moves along swiftly and effortlessly while we are deep and slow. Neither of us can be in the other's world, even though we share the seemingly same space, our road. We may as well be on other planets.

I remember after my brother died, when I was 19, I felt so much older than other people my age. And I would meet people along the way, the rest of my life, who had never lost a loved one to death, or who had never had deep trauma of any sort in their lives. It is a pleasure getting to know them, but there was no "place" for us to meet, to share from. Their perceptions of time, space and the world were so different from mine. Not better or worse, just different.

The emotional memory never leaves us. We continue to live and seemingly move on with our daily lives. We go back to work or school, meet new people and have new experiences. create and play, but at any moment, with the change of thought, we are back to that milestone. And if we cannot accept, forgive, and surrender, then what is truly happening is we are still back there and this daily life is only an act, and worldly time is only a stage for us to perform. Where we truly reside is in that past moment.

I believe in reality that this is what time is truly about; there is no past or future, there is only the present. And in the present moment we can be in the past and/or in the future. And I also believe this is why traumas of losing a loved one, being in accidents and getting injured badly, or being in war or other such profound events help us to begin to understand the true nature of life and spirituality. We stand at that pinnacle and view our life and the world from a whole new and deeper perspective. We, and everything around us, will never be quite the same.

I have heard it said that only when we give up a part of us do we truly grow. These events and experiences are pieces of ourselves, and from this point of view we are given huge growth and understanding from our difficulties. From this, we begin to understand that nothing is ultimately a tragedy or a negative experience, they are only events that happen in life that we must all go through, and are a part of this classroom in this world, where we gain knowledge and wisdom.

When you stand at this juncture, you turn to see that hope has been there with you all the time, but your eyes were clouded with emotion and confusion. Now you know that you and Hope walk together, always. Since you have met her and traveled with her, you can now take her everywhere and introduce her to others. Remember, they may not be able to see her yet, but the fact that you have been there for them with hope in their time of need means they will never be the same again. They have met her through your eyes, and in their own time, they will be able to know she is with them as well. After all, when you live with Hope, she has touched your heart and soul so that it is impossible to separate her from sharing her with others who are in despair. Despair is her shadow side, and you are there to shine the light on her so others may see reality: there is only Hope, not despair. It is all perception!

Death is not an event in life: we do not live to experience death. If we take eternity to mean not infinite temporal duration but timelessness, then eternal life belongs to those who live in the present.
(Ludwig Wittgenstein)

The shaman lives in a world where the Creator is not separate from the Creation, Heaven is not separate from Earth, and Spirit and matter infuse each other. The shaman does not believe in a division between the body and the spirit, or between the visible world of form and the invisible world of energy.

(Dr. Albert Villoldo)

*We are all but symbols of some greater thing—totems of ourselves—
subject to change and growth.
When we forget that metaphoric sense of ourselves, we lose sight of the overall path.*

(S. Kelley Harrell)

Part II

Symbols

My Symbols

Awake, awake O sleeper of the land of shadows. Awake. Expand!

(William Blake)

From the very beginning of my writing I have listened to inner voice, my "Tree of Life" or spirit from within to find my way. This entire book is a reflection of this process. I very rarely knew what I was doing except for the fact that I had a focus and a mission to accomplish and anything from that point was inner guidance to express the outer in matter. Many of the symbols I saw and used I later learned were archetypal in meaning. But it was always after the fact of them arriving in dreams and meditation or re-occurrences in my every day life that I would become aware of them. In my searching, I came upon what the ancients and man/womenkind have known for centuries. But herein lies the secret: I found them for myself and applied their meaning for my understanding of my mission for my life. Isn't that what all of us are to do? As with DNA, the structure is the same for all, but the pattern that is laid down gives us uniqueness. And isn't that what each life is about?

That which we do not bring to consciousness appears in our lives as fate.

(Carl Jung)

Archetypes

Jung talks about the archetype (also called "primordial image") as of biologists "patterns of behavior" (inborn behavior patterns). In short, archetypes are inborn tendencies which shape the human behavior.

(Carl Jung Resources)

I learned that nothing is new and that everything is made new by how we use and see the archetypes and applying our own specific experiences. This is what the archetype is meant to do. In the sameness we can find meaning for our uniqueness.

The archetypes, as unfiltered psychic experience, appear sometimes in their most primitive and naïve forms (in dreams), sometimes in a considerably more complex form due to the operation of conscious elaboration (in myths). Archetypal images expressed in religious dogma in particular are thoroughly elaborated into formalized structures which, while by expressing the unconscious in a circuitous manner, prevent direct confrontation with it.

(Carl Jung)

*An **archetype** is a universally understood symbol, term, statement, or pattern of behavior. A prototype upon which others are copied, patterned, or emulated. Archetypes are often used in myths and storytelling across different cultures.
In psychology, an archetype is a model of a person, personality, or behavior.*

(Wikipedia)

It is an exciting and exhilarating experience to come to a conclusion or perception and then through study or chance realize all you have done is to tap into the subconscious, the mass consciousness of man or to your very own spiral of knowledge deep inside of you. It is our ego that tells us that we have the answers to something new and wonderful. The truth is, all knowledge is known by everyone, it is only discovered or seen by you. That is why you will hear of several discoveries or new waves of thought coming out into the public mind at once. It is as if the spirit leads certain individuals as instruments to get across a concept of ideas to express in matter at that place and time. So what happens is several people will be speaking about the same subject in different cultures and places. It is as if it is time for all people to hear and see.

But what is the archetype? A hereditary gift which moulds and transforms the individual consciousness. A fact defined more through a tendency than through specific inherited contents, images, etc.; a matrix which influences the human behavior as well as his ideas and concepts on the ethical, moral, religious and cultural levels. Jung talks about the archetype (also called 'primordial image') as of biologists' patterns of behavior (inborn behavior patterns). In short, archetypes are inborn tendencies which shape the human behavior.

(Carl Jung Resources)

...the archetype of initiation is strongly activated to provide a meaningful transition...with a rite of passage from one stage of life to the next,' such stages may include being parented, initiation, courtship, marriage and preparation for death.

(Wikipedia)

Some archetypes (of the collective unconscious) are: the Hero, the Martyr, the Great Mother, the Wise Sage, the Warrior, the Trickster, the Wise Old Woman or Man.

Carl Jung gave us these main archetypes:

The SELF: the self is an archetype that represents the unification of the unconsciousness and consciousness of an individual.

The SHADOW: the shadow is an archetype that consists of the sex and life instincts. It is the dark place we do not show to ourselves, let alone the world.

The ANIMA and ANIMUS: the female has a male aspect in the psyche that is the animus. The male has a female aspect and that is the anima. These represent the "true self" rather than the image we present to others. It serves as the primary source of communication with the collective unconscious.

The PERSONA: the persona is how we present ourselves to the world. In Latin persona means mask.

Before Jung there was Plato who spoke of archetypes. From Wikipedia: *"Plato's ideas were pure mental forms that were imprinted in the soul before it was born into the world. They were collective in the sense that they embodied the fundamental characteristics of a thing rather than its specific peculiarities."*

The Greeks believed in the "Gods" and today we call them myths. These Gods and Goddesses are archetypes. Some of these are Zeus, Apollo, Hades, Demeter, Athena and more. In the upcoming pages you will see how these Goddesses gave me back my hope.

The Oriental archetypes can be quite different. There is the belief that everything comes from the "unnamable." In watching nature we see the flow of life for humans as well as nature. The five elements: wood, fire, earth, metal, water are all important to the psyche as well as in Chinese medicine. These archetypes symbolize character aspect of a person. For example: wood is attributed to male energy and means strength. It is leadership and assertive qualities.

An author and scholar whom I read during my time of searching in the dark was Joseph Campbell. He believed that the archetype of the Hero was the biggest part of our psyches. Campbell said *"A hero ventures forth from the world of the common day into a region of supernatural wonder: fabulous forces are there encountered and a decisive victory is won; the hero comes back from this mysterious adventure with the power to bestow boons on his fellow man."* Campbell's quote could not be a better explanation of my journey and I think it hits the nail on the head for most of us. *"That's the thing with magic. You've got to know it's still here, all around us, or it just stays invisible for you." (Charles de Lint)*

I believe it is now time for the entire world to truly know that HOPE is eternal and that by this message we can transform our lives to a healthier and happier, more loving state of being.

What kinds of Archetype do you identify with at this present time and why? During a stage of transition or at a time of great loss, what kind of Archetype stood out for you and how did it help you to see your situation in a new light?

The Front Cover

The Four Corners of Hope

The Matter of Hope symbol, as seen above, came in my sleep and each piece revealed itself slowly to me. The divider of the circle is the cross. It is has equal cross bars but it is a cross just the same. This is the symbol for matter. The cross in the circle, I later learned, represents the interweaving of energy that brings form in the physical plane. The horizontal line is the earthly plane and the vertical is spirit coming to the earthly plane, into matter. It can also be seen as the Eastern cultures claim, the Yin and the Yang, or the female and male. And when we come together as male and female we create new beings from our love, in matter.

Each tribe or group of people creates mandalas or circular images that symbolize the sacred or their beliefs from their perceptions. Each of us has a perception of the world and groups hold beliefs and perceptions, as well. This symbol is my Mandela for The Matter of Hope.

I live in Arizona. In the Eastern upper corner of our state there is a place called the four corners. This is where four states meet one another and is the only place in the United States that this happens. It is interesting that it sits on Native American ground and between, or near, several different tribes.

Native American spirituality uses the four directions, North, South, East and West when worshipping. The medicine wheel is used in some tribes'/nations' ceremonies to represent these forces. They say that powerful energy forces can be raised as people gather around one of these wheels. The four directions are known throughout time and cultures as a universal archetype. This concept is what is seen in the four states that meet: Arizona, Southwest; Utah, Northwest; Colorado, Northeast and New Mexico, Southeast. This is not the pure directions as in the Native culture but I still find it interesting that this geographic location sits on land of a people that hold respect for the these forces. On the front of this book is the circle with the four sections as seen in the Native American and other cultures, such as the Celts. What follows is why I selected this symbol. Although I had some knowledge before I choose the symbol, I learned much more after I selected it.

I woke up one morning with the cover in my mind. It was to be a symbol. It is symbols that can speak to the deepest parts of us. Jung used symbols in all his work, dreams, ancient symbols or archetypes all interested him in exploring our subconscious mind.

This time more was revealed in relationship to the writing of The Matter of Hope. Lo and behold, in many tribes and cultures the circle represents mother and Mother Earth. The actual circular form is the womb from where all life comes. You must realize I was not aware of these new definitions until a year after placing it on the front cover. As I saw it, it was first my womb holding my child Hope. Second, it was the universal symbol for us all and Mother Earth bringing of Hope into matter. I was unaware of the meanings of what I had drawn on the front cover but I did not seek out the meaning. I happened on to this information by sheer accident. However, as you will find out later there are no accidents, only synchronicity.

Numbers are the universal language. Mathematics is everything. It is in every atom and concept in the universe. Mathematics are the building blocks of creation. It is how science can let us understand how we got here, how we are made.

Number "four" kept popping up as I searched for my understanding of hope. In fact, much of my writing starts with numbers in my head; funny thing for a girl who hated math in school. I see things like this, see or make out symbols and then they seem to translate into numbers. It comes to me like this, in numbers to concepts and concepts to thought and language. So number four brings to mind the "four corners" of traditional buildings. It is the symbol for building and holding up a structure—foundation. Even the foundation of our DNA is four elements; carbon, oxygen, hydrogen and nitrogen. It is amazing that what we are made of is the same as what the planets and majority of the universe is made of; the same stuff as the stars. That in itself can give you hope. It makes me smile.

We ourselves are made of stardust.
(Carl Sagan)

Seriously, it makes you think where did these elements come from and why? In his book *How to Know God* Deepak Chopra talks about creation:

The power of creation—whatever it turns out to be—lies even beyond energy, a force with the ability to turn gaseous clouds of dust into stars and eventually into DNA.

In the Hebrew tradition each letter is given a number. The letter, Daleth, is given the number four and it is considered the "Door". This is a major section in the Kabbalah. The Kabbalah is an ancient Jewish tradition. Some call it the Tree of Knowledge or "Wisdom of Truth". The Kabbalah is a path of discipline that leads to the Divine. It also tells us how we and the Universe were created by a "Descent of Power" through a series of energy flows top to bottom in the shape of a spiral. Daleth is an area on the tree. Some say it is an abyss between the higher concepts and the highest spiritual realm. In the Kabbalah it comes just before your consciousness crosses into to wisdom and understanding, finally seeing God, or the virtual state. There are four worlds within the Kabbalah or four trees of life. They are form, patterns, archetypes and activity. Also on the tree of life the fourth emanation is Love and Mercy. Finally, there are four major areas to us; physical, mental, emotional, and spiritual.

In our lives there is a single color, as on an artist's palette, which provides the meaning of life and art. it is the color of love.
(Marc Chagall)

Then there were the colors. Colors are very hard to tie down. They mean so many different things to many different groups. It is all in the perception of the group and the location of the group how they interpret the meaning of colors. For example, red can mean anger or the sun, or to some it is love and passion. White can mean purity or totality to some people. In the East, women dress in red on their wedding day, but if we in the West dressed in red the bride would be thought of as if she were a fallen woman. So color is very much in how we perceive our world and our culture. Once again, depending on which American Indian tribe you look at, they will tell you different meanings for each color. Some will say the red is the sun and the south, when another tribe in another region of the country will say green is the south. In England violet or purple is a sign of royalty. The colors of the seven rays in the Eastern traditions attribute various states of being and consciousness. These in turn relate to the seven major chakras.

Chakra is a concept referring to wheel-like vortices which, according to traditional Indian medicine, are believed to exist in the surface of the subtle body of living beings. The Chakras are said to be 'force centers' or whorls of energy permeating, from a point on the physical body, the layers of the subtle bodies in an ever-increasing fan-shaped formation. Rotating vortices of subtle matter, they are considered the focal points for the reception and transmission of energies. Different systems posit a varying number of chakras; the most well known system in the West is that of seven chakras.

(Wikipedia)

The chakra system has red, yellow, green, blue, indigo and violet to represent the points on the body.

Our eyes receive the light that gives us the colors that we see. Without light there is no color. White light from the sun is all colors. We see color because our eyes have light receptors in them. Each receptor is sensitive to different wavelengths of light. There may be variations among individuals in these receptors. One kind of color blindness, for example, is the inability to differentiate between red and green light; there is no difference in perception. The primary colors of additive light are red, blue, and green and the secondary are yellow, cyan and magenta. Black is the base and light is "added" to eventually get to white; all colors together. This is the science of additive color in a nutshell.

Color has everything to do with light. When the sun shines through a prism or the sunshine through rain drops one gets a rainbow. How our eyes receive the light gives us the colors that we see. Light itself has no color.

Visible light is the part of the electromagnetic spectrum that our eyes can see. Light from the sun or a light bulb may look white, but it is actually a combination of many colors. We can see the different colors of the spectrum by splitting the light with a prism. The spectrum is also visible when you see a rainbow in the sky.

(sciencemadesimple.com)

The symbol of the rainbow means many things to many people. Christians see the rainbow as a promise from God.

Here is the definition of rainbows:

Rainbows
a. An arc of spectral colors, usually identified as red, orange, yellow, green, blue, indigo, and violet, that appears in the sky opposite the sun as a result of the refractive dispersion of sunlight in drops of rain or mist.
b. A similar arc or band, as one produced by a prism or by iridescence.
c. A graded display of colors.
d. An illusory hope: *chasing the rainbow of overnight success.*

(www.answers.com)

James Gurney tells us "*The Greeks believed the rainbow was a path between the earth and heaven. In Norse mythology the rainbow was seen as a bridge between Ásgard and Midgard, the realms of the gods and mankind respectively. In Chinese mythology, the rainbow was regarded as as a slit in the sky sealed with stones of five different colors.*"

Arthur Weinberg says about the rainbow: "*A token means a sign and a covenant is a agreement. So whenever we see a rainbow this is a sign of God's promise never to destroy the earth and to always teach us His ways through His Manifestations. In Muslim tradition, we are told that God made all people out of seven different colored earths. This teaches us that the earth belongs to all people, no matter what their color, and not to any one special race. Just as the seven colors of the Spectrum join to make one light, so the different colored races must join to make One Human family.*" The examples of what colors mean are endless. So where we stand on the circle of the family of earth will give us varying degrees of understanding of color.

The Matter of Hope colors are black, red, white and yellow: white for **peace and awareness**, yellow for **tranquility and empathy**, black for **balance and understanding**. For me, the red stands for **harmony and interconnectedness** of the universe and each other. It is the carnal, earthly parts of us as matter expressed in a positive way. And the four colors also symbolize the racial colors of humans on the planet. As we search for hope, these qualities will be integral parts of the quest.

The use of color and designs to symbolize ideals, thoughts and beliefs frees the right brain from the left brain to help heal the wounds of loss. Sometimes events or ideas become too overwhelming for us to understand, so symbols help the mind to relax so that meaning can arise from someplace other than logic. In our travels looking for the meaning of hope, we need to gaze upon symbols and listen to myths for deeper understanding.

When you look at a map you will find the four directions: North, South, East, and West. And when you go from one point to the other to unite these places on the map, you create a circle. Stand at any point and you will always have a direction in front of you, behind you, to your left and to your right. It is your choice which way to go or to stand still, but one fact remains, no matter which way you proceed, once you stop again the cycle starts all over. It is always the never ending same four directions, and the same choices are present; which way do you go? It is the circle of life and the choices of which way do you follow that never changes. There are always at least four choices for you to move toward, and when you realize the never ending selection of varying degrees of directions, the possibilities are limitless.

So it is as we take our journey in search of hope. How do we know which way to go? How will we know there is anything but grief at the end of the path? Will we just go in circles with no answer?

The nature of God is a circle of which the Center is everywhere and the circumference is nowhere.
(Empedocles)

The circle is the never ending cycle. Inside of it is a meeting point where spirit meets matter, and past meets the future in the present. When they meet birth and death are one and there is no more loss. It is where the poet is the scientist and the artist is an engineer, where the creator creates himself and it is us. It is the place where the mother of us all holds us in her hand and where we may rest in protection, compassion, and faith. In the palm of her hand, at the center, is HOPE.

And the way to find Hope is through the spiral. Within our own physical body is the antenna to the Universe. It is the double helix of our DNA, of all knowledge and Hope.

When we see something our eyes relay the image to the brain. The brain labels and identifies what information the eye has given it. Sometimes the brain has a difficult time perceiving what it is seeing. It searches for meaning. With optical illusions it teaches our brain and eyes to shift and switch back and forth looking at the same thing in a different way. This process and experience could then help us by translating into how we think or perceive life. What do you see below?

As I was doing my final proofing on this material, I looked away from my computer and fixed my gaze on the cover of the book. It was sitting on the floor to the right of my chair. Why didn't I get this before now?! It is a human. It is you and it is me. The symbol is all I spoke of in this section, but I now could see the true meaning. If you look at the symbol from an aerial view one can see it all. The rainbow is the chakras system surrounding us. The cross is spirit into matter which brings us into this world. The four colors are the four races (select one!), and finally the spiral of our DNA.

Symbols are magical. They remain stationary, but over time our perceptions and perspective will change so the symbol will reveal new meaning. My symbol began to speak. It became alive to me. Because I am about to give birth to this body of work, I believe I was able to finally see what the symbol truly meant. You and I are the symbols of Hope in Matter.

Perception and Perspective

The tragic or the humorous is a matter of perspective.

(Arnold Beisser)

How we see and view things can be determined by where we stand in life. This means how we were raised, culture, and education, as well as, how we were treated by others in the past and present, gives a perception and perspective on life. We all see things a little differently. If you lived in a community where children were honored and loved you may have a very positive perspective about children. However, if you lived in a place where children were in the way and not respected, you may have views that are similar. Other times we make sure we think the opposite of how we were treated or how we lived.

How we see life comes from where we stood or are standing.

The following is a metaphor for us to understand these concepts and can help us change unwanted perceptions.

On the following pages you will be asked to draw lines and circles. By doing this exercise you begin to see how perceptions can change from where you stand at any point on a line or in a circle.

Exercise:

Stand in the center of a room. Look around. Note all the areas of the room. Stand and take note of what you see.

Now, move to a corner of the room. Take note of what you see.

Move yet to another area of the room. What do you see?

How does the room vary from each place you stand?

When we decorate our rooms or rearrange we do this to see how we can make a room more beautiful. I am asking you to compare how differently it appears from where you stand.

The point is, when we take a new look at a subject or at our lives it can make a big change in how we feel and understand things. As you move through this workbook you will need to do just that; move into new territory in your mind.

Everything we hear is an opinion, not a fact. Everything we see is a perspective, not the truth.

(Marcus Aurelius)

It Is All in How You Look at It!

"If we are always arriving and departing, it is also true that we are eternally anchored. One's destination is never a place but rather a new way of looking at things."

(Henry Miller)

The myth of Pandora's Box is the metaphor for the fact that all of mankind suffers.

If we recognize our suffering it then can mean the beginning of the end to it.

We do understand we all suffer, many times we refuse to see that truth; denial of this fact makes the suffering worse. Some of us remain in it for years, afraid to face the fact.

*If the doors of perception were cleansed,
man would see everything as it is, infinite.*

(William Blake)

We must become aware and then give as much compassion to ourselves or to others who are suffering. Empathy unites us and shows us how interconnected we are. We are not alone.

We are taught when we feel pain or suffering to brush it away, instead of thinking on that pain and suffering.

EXERCISE:

In your mind do the following visualization.

(Close your eyes. If you are doing this on your own have a friend you trust read the following to you, slowly and gently, or read beforehand and try to remember.)

Think of some pain or suffering in your life.
Now become fully aware of it. Think about it for a few seconds. Know you are safe and look at it without fear.

Think of it as a symbol. See it. Name it.
What is happening in your body and mind as you transform it into a symbol?

Take the symbol and lay it on the ground outside. Now walk away from the symbol.

See a big hill. Begin walking up the hill. When you have reached half way up the hill turn around and look down at that symbol of suffering.
From that perspective what does it look like?

Has it totally changed into a new symbol? Has it become smaller or misshapen?
From this new view, how does your mind and body feel?

Do you get new insights or new feelings? Is the suffering or pain less?

As you think of this take note. Now turn and walk up the hill to the highest point. Go as far you can. Go where you can no longer see the symbol of your pain.

Turn and look down at the symbol. You can no longer see it.
Now gently remove and release it in you mind and heart. Release the pain that goes along with the suffering. Let the pain drift off into the sky. Feel a gentle breeze as you do this and know that breeze represents compassion for yourself.

Stand and notice how your body feels after the withdrawal from the suffering. Feel the breeze all over you body. Relax and accept the gentle feeling of compassion. Emotionally, how does it feel to release all the pain?

Now look around and see that others are on their own hills doing the same thing. You acknowledge each other and you all know you are not alone in this venture.

Knowing this fact, slowly move down the hill. Go right past where your symbol was laying and greet the others. Know that each of them has done the same job but in their own mind. Feel the comfort and compassion in this fact. You are connected in this way.

Take a deep breathe and remember the breeze that brought compassion.

Open your eyes. How does the suffering feel now?

Focus now on one of these: AWARENESS, COMPASSION, EMPATHY and INTERCONNECTEDNESS.

Please write about your experience during this exercise.

"Whatever you perceive through the senses or the mind, there is nothing lasting about it, it is just movement. It is the attention given to it that gives it the sense of reality."

(Mooji)

Begin with a Point

Draw a line horizontally in each direction from this dot.

●

Next draw a line as you did above then draw another line vertically through the dot to form a cross.

●

Make the cross, and then draw two new lines diagonally.

●

This exercise is meant to help the mind to begin to view things in a different way. Using a symbol instead of words, your mind and brain have to travel to a new place. Symbols are all around us in daily life. We have become used to them. Then there are the ancient symbols that we have used and seen over and over again without thought of their original meaning. We know that the simple shapes have been the earliest form of communication for man. The point or dot, for example, means the Self; it also means God. So in the exercise the dot is you, the lines are the ways to look at a problem or any situation.

In the circle below place a dot in the center.

Next draw as many lines through the dot as you can.

When you are finished, in your mind try seeing the circle with all the lines in it, as a 3 dimensional object.

Try to find an object you can hold that is a spherical shape, such as an apple or a small ball. Move it around in your hands and look at it from all sides. Imagine if it had lines through the entire object.

The lines represent points of view. This exercise is to help you to look at simple shapes from a new perspective. There are so many ways to look at an object, so many dimensions.

It is the same with our thoughts and how we look at the world or our problems. This type of experience can help you to exercise your mind in looking for new solutions. Each line represents a new way of doing or seeing a problem. POSSIBILITIES ARE UNLIMITED. THIS IS HOPE.

The cross is: matter, or the four directions (in the southwest you see many crosses on the walls of canyons; this means the four directions).

From About.com:
Crosses very commonly represent the earth and the physical universe, particularly in Western culture. This comes primarily from two associations: the four physical elements (earth, water, air and fire) and the four cardinal directions (north, south, east and west). The same symbol is also known as a sun cross or solar wheel and has been associated with the sun and its four seasons.

The horizontal line has represented the earthly plain and the vertical the spiritual plane. The apex is the bringing spirit into matter.

Circle is: the union of things, season and cycles.

From www.whats-your-sign.com:

The circle symbol meaning is universal, sacred and divine. It represents the infinite nature of energy, and the inclusivity of the universe.

These are only a few of many of our ordinary shapes and what they symbolize. Symbols help us see things in a new way as with the drawing of the lines. It is another language; a way the brain can think or communicate new thoughts. It is the subconscious or the spiritual self speaking to us.

Try to think of three symbols you use in your life. Write them and why do your use them?

Example: I draw a silly little face when I write a note to my son instead of my signing MOM.

This week try to become aware of symbols around you. And question their meaning.

The Mandala of Hope

man da la [muhn-dl-uh] noun 1. Oriental Art. a schematized representation of the cosmos, chiefly characterized by a concentric configuration of geometric shapes, each of which contains an image of a deity or an attribute of a deity. 2. (in Jungian psychology) a symbol representing the effort to reunify the self.

(Dictionary.com)

WE NEED SYMBOLS AROUND US TO REMIND US OF HOPE.

Everyday we use symbols without even thinking about it. The dollar sign, $, is a symbol and so is the sign at the cross walk of the little man walking or the hand for "do not walk". The Christian cross or the Jewish star are all symbols we see each and everyday and think nothing of it. The dictionary tells us: A symbol **is something chosen to represent something else. An object to typify a quality, abstract idea; for example, the oak is a symbol of strength.**

Symbols run much deeper than we realize. The psychologists tell us symbols, in matter or physical state, serve for spiritual realities. With this meaning isn't our physical body only a symbol of spirit?

Symbols were the first language and letters are symbols that we now know as language. From Carl Jung's book, *Man and His Symbols*, he says: *"As the mind explores the symbols, it is led to ideas that lie beyond the grasp of reason."*

Jung believed that Mandalas helped humans heal. By creating our own symbols with a focus in mind and through a kind of meditative state while drawing, one can integrate a kind of mystical joining of the lower into higher states of being. We become aware of many different facets of ourselves and at the same time our awareness unifies and creates wholeness.

When you think of the concept of Hope what do you see?

What is a symbol of Hope for you? Why? Write this.

Instructions for Making a Mandala

Now in the space below you will see a circle. In this circle I would like you to draw your Symbol of Hope. This is your Mandala. Before you begin I will give you instructions on how to begin. You may use any tools and colors your heart desires. This YOU, for you to use now and in the future to meditate on, contemplate, and remind you of your place of hope. See the following page for instructions.

When you are making your Mandala do not use words. A mandala is a visual symbol.
Use pencil to start with but have markers, canyons, paints, or any other materials to make color.
1. Find a time when you have no interruptions and are free to create and express yourself. Please be alone and quiet to do this.
2. Turn off the radio and TV, but if you would like to play some music it may enhance the process.
3. Start by sitting in a comfortable position and just letting everything go in your mind. Close your eyes. Breathe normally first and then do the deep breathing.
4. Begin to concentrate on what you wrote about your symbol of hope. Think it first. Now see it. What does it look like?
5. Keep breathing and totally focus on the concept of Hope and what it means to you. After about 5 minutes open your eyes and begin to draw.
6. In pencil make a dot in the middle of the circle.
7. Ask your inner voice for guidance in helping you create. You may now be seeing flashes of color or shapes, or you may not see anything. Focus on the color first. What is the first color that comes to mind when you think of Hope?
8. Now begin from the center of the circle moving outward and begin to put in your colors and shapes. When symbols come to you it may come quickly and you will be drawing fast and furiously. Try not to think anything is stupid or silly, that is the left brain telling you old patterns of things about being perfect or conforming. That is not why you are doing this. This should come from deep inside of you. Let yourself go.
9. Now you will be filling this circle with any combinations of shapes, colors, pictures that represent hope for you.
10. After about 30 minutes you may feel as if you are done. You may go on or stop for now. As the days progress you may find yourself thinking back and wanting to add to your mandala, this is great. It is an ongoing creation.
11. After about a week, finish. Hang it in a place where you can see it each day. This is your reminder that you have Hope in your life, that you have made the Matter of Hope for yourself. Well done!

Letting Hope Fly

After you have drawn Your Symbol of Hope you will be asked to use it. By that I mean, hang it somewhere inside, or better yet, outside on your patio or in a tree. There is a practice in many cultures where people make symbols of positive thoughts and prayers that they then let fly in the wind.

There are the Prayer Flags of Tibet:

Prayer Flags are inscribed with auspicious symbols, invocations, prayers, and mantras. Tibetan Buddhists for centuries have planted these flags outside their homes and places of spiritual practice for the wind to carry the beneficent vibrations across the countryside. Prayer flags are said to bring happiness, long life and prosperity to the flag planter and those in the vicinity.

(www.prayerflags.com)

All over the world people make objects to send prayers and positive thoughts out into the Universe to the Creator or God. In the Hopi Native American tradition, one of these is a Bahos (pahos) or a prayer carrier. During a Hopi ceremony the Bahos is tied to things. They are tied to ladders to prevent accidents, a sheep to increase the herd, or a fruit tree to have a larger crop.

Prayer Ties hold our heart and as the Prayer Ties are released, they carry our desires to the Creators.

(Eagle Spirit Ministry)

By creating your symbol on paper and placing it in "matter" you can now let it go. You can see it daily and feel what you created and let it work in your life. LET HOPE FLY!

Rise above sectional interests and private ambitions...
Pass from Matter to spirit is diversity; spirit is light, life and unity.
(Muhammad Iqbal)

Mythology is the womb of mankind's initiation to life and death.
(Joseph Campbell)

Part III

The Matter of the Myth and Archetype

Myths Can Help Us Heal

If you live with the myths in your mind, you will find yourself always in mythological situations. They cover everything that can happen to you. And that enables you to interpret the myth in relation to life, as well as life in relation to myth.

(Joseph Campbell, to Michael McKnight)

Myths are stories. They are stories that are based on legends that have a deep symbolic meaning for all people. For those who tell it and hear it, it somehow conveys the truth instead of just recounting the story for its events. Some myths are actual events that happened in real life but because of their intense actions they become transformed in symbolic meanings or are changed in time and space. They are used to explain universal beginnings and sometimes involve supernatural beings. The power of the myth, to a culture in which they are developed, is a major reason why they survive as long as they do, sometimes for thousands of years.

These stories have archetypical characters that make up the central theme. An archetype comes from the human psyche, the unconscious. The human psyche is the same all over the world; who knows, maybe the psyche goes as deep as into the DNA, because no matter where we are the body has the same impulses and instincts.

Shakespeare said that art is a mirror held up to nature. And that's what it is. The nature is your nature, and all of these wonderful poetic images of mythology are referring to something in you. When your mind is simply trapped by the image out there so that you never make the reference to yourself, you have misread the image.
The inner world is the world of your requirements and your energies and your structure and your possibilities that meets the outer world. And the outer world is the field of your incarnation. That's where you are. You've got to keep both going. As Novalis said, "The seat of the soul is there where the inner and outer worlds meet."

(Joseph Campbell)

A myth in the truest sense is inspiring. When do we need inspiration more than when we have lost someone or something that we love or has immense value? And yet in these times nothing seems to break through to inspire and touch us. We feel lost ourselves and that a part of us has died, so we are essentially asleep. We feel as if we are dreaming while we are wide awake. In these moments in our lives only the voice of the poet and story teller can be heard. We may listen to a story that we think will ease our pain and it will take us away, only to find out that like Alice falling down the rabbit hole we are taken by surprise by how easily we are hypnotized by the events being told, and magically the story teller is talking about our own life. It transcends all thought. This is inspiration from the myth.

Wait for me, Mr. White Rabbit. I'm coming, too! [Falling] How curious. I never realized that rabbit holes were so dark . . . and so long . . . and so empty. I believe I have been falling for five minutes, and I still can't see the bottom! Hmph! After such a fall as this, I shall think nothing of tumbling downstairs. How brave they'll all think me at home. Why, I wouldn't say anything about it even if I fell off the top of the house! I wonder how many miles I've fallen by this time. I must be getting somewhere near the center of the earth. I wonder if I shall fall right through the earth! How funny that would be. Oh, I think I see the bottom. Yes, I'm sure I see the bottom. I shall hit the bottom, hit it very hard, and oh, how it will hurt!

(Lewis Carroll)

Alice knows there is a bottom; so shall we know that through that dark hole there is a bottom of acceptance of what has happened and it hurts. However, the fall is over and we can stand and go on to finding new life and hope. So it is through stories, myths and symbols that we connect our hearts and spirits once more with our mind.

As I stated above these experiences and stories transcend thought.

A ritual is the enactment of a myth. And, by participating in the ritual, you are participating in the myth. And since myth is a projection of the depth wisdom of the psyche, by participating in a ritual, participating in the myth, you are being, as it were, put in accord with that wisdom, which is the wisdom that is inherent within you anyhow. Your consciousness is being re-minded of the wisdom of your own life.

I think ritual is terribly important.
(Joseph Campbell, interview with Michael Toms)

When I was younger I was rebellious and poo-pooed ritual. I felt it too strict, stiff, and restricting for me as a child and young adult. But it was as if ritual was finding me. And I learned to respect and honor how important ritual is to our lives.

A few days after my brother passed away I was to open in a college play, *Dandelion Wine*. My parents and I spoke about how Greg would have wanted me to go on with the play…so I did. Not until I walked on stage and sat in the rocking chair in the spot light did I realize what I was about to do. I could not back out now and I got into character. I was the great grandmother in the story and I was giving a speech about dying, and then I died. At my feet sat the character of my grandson, Doug, who was in reality my old boyfriend from high school, Larry. Larry was the one who came to my college classroom only a few days earlier to tell me the news about my brother. There we sat, just he and I in character, with him looking up at me, all along knowing what I had just experienced in my real life.

I guess, I did the piece just fine and I could hear the entire audience sobbing because many knew my real life situation. Great Grandma says "*Don't want anyone saying sweet things about me; I said it all in my time and my pride. I've tasted every victual and danced every dance; now there's one last tart I haven't bit on, one tune I haven't whistled. But I'm not afraid. I'm truly curious. Death won't get a crumb by my mouth I won't keep and savor. So don't you worry over me. Now, go, and let me find my sleep….*" (Ray Bradbury, *Dandelion Wine*).

This was a ritual for me and the audience. It was not planned, but none the less it was cathartic for me and those present. It feels like a dream now but it did happen.

As Joseph Campbell writes: "*By participating in a ritual, participating in the myth, you are being, as it were, put in accord with that wisdom, which is the wisdom that is inherent within you anyhow. Your consciousness is being re-minded of the wisdom of your own life.*"

What rituals can you think of for you to enact the myth that symbolizes your life experiences with the loss of hope or your losses?

Myths are metaphors. What metaphors fits your life and its dramas and tragedies?

The Myth of Hope

The story of Hope goes something like this; Pandora, whose name means "all gifts", was created by Zeus and Hephaestus in ancient Greece. She was created by these Gods to punish the human race. She was the first woman given to man and was fashioned after a goddess. (Sounds like the biblical Adam and Eve story so far.)

All the Gods and Goddesses came forward to give her gifts. She was given beauty, cunning, grace, and dexterity, to name a few of the positive ones. She was also given deceit and lying. Finally, she was presented to Epimetheus as a gift. Prometheus, his brother, had just given mankind fire before Pandora was created. He warned his brother to never take gifts from Zeus, but Epimetheus was taken by Pandora's beauty and forgot. She brought with her a covered earthen vessel. Pandora had been told by Zeus to never open the vessel, but curiosity got the better of her and she opened it. Out poured all the struggles, pain, and sorrows of mankind. Pandora was horrified to watch all of them fly out the window to spread over the world. She could not stop those that escaped but hurried to put the lid on to trap the one last occupant of the vessel. It was Elpis, or Hope. Elpis was put there to remind humans that no matter how bad things became, there is always Hope.

Another account of the story is that Pandora took the vessel to her man and convinced him to open it. This time it was only benefits that poured out, but the lid was put on and Hope remained inside.

In Rome she was later known as Spes, the goddess of Hope. She was seen as the Goddess of the underworld, or the subconscious, and she was the cousin of death and sleep. Statues could be seen in the temples of her holding a cornucopia, or the horn of plenty, and in the other hand, a bunch of poppies. She represents a very old concept, as early as from the 4th century B.C., but little more is known of her. It will be our job to learn for ourselves who and what she is for us.

Another account of the story in Roman mythology has Spes as the personification of Hope. Originally, being a nature goddess (like Venus the garden goddess with whom she was sometimes identified), she represented the hope of fruitful gardens and fields, then of abundant offspring, and lastly of prosperity to come and good fortune in general; hence, she was invoked on birthdays and at weddings. Of her numerous temples in Rome, the most ancient was appropriately in the vegetable market built during the first Punic war. Since that time it was twice burnt down and restored. The day of its dedication (August 1st) corresponds with the birthday of Claudius, which explains the frequent occurrence of Spes on the coins of that emperor. Spes is represented as a beautiful maiden in a long light robe, lifting up her skirt with her left hand, and carrying in her right hand a closed bud about to open. Sometimes, she wears a garland of flowers on her head and ears of corn and poppy heads in her hand, which are symbolical of a prosperous harvest. Like Fortune, with whom she is often coupled in inscriptions on Roman tombstones, she was also represented with the cornucopia (horn of plenty).

Why did we named our daughter Hope? Because we made the decision to name her after a concept that I held in the highest regard in my life I was forced to look at what this all meant to me and where I was to go with it. I had lost both my daughter and my life mission. These myths helped me in my grief. Hope was named after this concept that people told me I processed. And as I learned the history and origins of the concept the more it made sense. Like the vessel that held all the horrifying things of earth Hope stayed at the bottom. She stayed there because no matter how bad things got we were to remember there is always hope. Not even death could take hope away. I read about Spes and how she was the cousin to sleep and death, this made more sense now. I felt as if I was living some kind of myth. After all, what is a myth but someone's story, and my story was too unbelievable even for me to feel and understand as I lived it.

Change is a constant companion. What we can really count on is CHANGE. That is what death and life is about: one change after the other. When we have attachment to someone or something, we will suffer, because there is nothing that stays forever except change. If we only rely on things and people, we will lose all hope because things wear out and people have their own free will. AA and 12 step programs are based on this theory, "..we have no control over people, places, or things."

Practice detachment in all of these, **and have faith** in something bigger than yourself and **have faith in yourself.**

If you are, as the old saying goes, "dangling on one thin thread of hope," you still have HOPE. Faith is holding hope up, and it is your love and the compassion of the universe that can turn the tide. Remember, "*Elpis was put there to remind humans that no matter how bad things became, there is always Hope.*" Think then on the bud of a flower about to open.

Write a short story about when you first lost hope. Does your story fit one of the myths or in history? Who and what do you identify with in any legend or myth?

A Myth of Life and Death

**Both dreams and myths are important communications
from ourselves to ourselves. If we do not understand
the language in which they are written, we miss a great deal of what we know and tell ourselves in
those hours when we are not busy manipulating the outside world.**

(Erich Fromm, Ph.D.)

Demeter and Persephone

Zeus and Demeter had a daughter, Kore. Demeter was the mother of all plant life on earth and was considered the Queen of earth and Zeus the King of heaven.

There were no seasons, no winter, no summer, and no fall. It was as if spring was forever. Leaves, vines, flowers, and all crops were growing all the time. It was paradise.

Then one day Kore was playing with her friends on the hillside—young maidens running through the meadows of flowers in full innocence and bliss.

From the underworld came the God Hades. He needed a mate. He snapped up Kore knowing she was the Goddess daughter of the two most powerful Gods. No one heard her screams but the Goddess Hecate.

Demeter was frantic and looked everywhere for nine days. But she could not find her beloved daughter. Then Hecate told her she had heard screams.

Demeter decided to take a mortal form in hopes she could be closer to her daughter. She worked for a woman taking care of her newborn son. Demeter was to nurse the child, but she gave him the food of gods instead. She was going to place him in the fire as the last purification to becoming a god, when the child's mother walked in, horrified. Demeter yelled at the woman for stopping her, for now the child was dead and not immortal.

She demanded a temple be built in her daughter's honor. Then she sent a plague upon the earth and nothing grew. Man was going to starve unless she could see her daughter.

Zeus stepped in and ordered his daughter, Kore, to come back. No longer called Kore, Demeter's daughter was now named Persephone, Queen of the Underworld. Demeter had refused to go back to the mountain of the Gods or even talk with the other Gods until she could see her daughter Persephone again.

Hades told his bride, Persephone, that she could go if she ate the seeds of the pomegranate. This made it so she could never stay at her mother's side and would have to return to him. She was allowed to stay with the other Gods for only nine months, then for three she had to go back underground.

So that was how winter was born. Three months of the year Demeter is sad and lonely for her daughter, but then she appears to be by her side the rest of the year. Demeter then allows the plants to grow and the land is fertile once again.

This myth is full of metaphors and layers of life lessons. The two goddesses represent the two major opposite aspects of the psyche struggling to maintain control.

Their myth represents, among other things, an attempt to see the whole momentous relationship of the higher and lower, the light and the dark worlds, as part of a dynamic relationship a cycle of life and death in which all beings participate.
(Jennifer Barker Woolger and Roger J. Woolger)

We, as a nation, went through our own terror and deep journey to the underworld on September 11, 2001. There is almost no need for any more myths like those of Demeter and Persephone; our experience has been enough. We are mourning this loss. Like Demeter wandering the earth looking for her lost daughter, we too wander yearning for the time before the attack, the time before the loss of the lives of our loved ones. Life will never be the same. The anniversary, like any death anniversary, allows us to return to that time to try and make sense of the loss.

As time goes by, there will be signs of rebirth, although we will never have our loved ones again. At some point, they will re-emerge through memories, in books about them, children born to them becoming successful, buildings built in their memory, music written about them, and the list goes on and on. Unfortunately, they will not return for three months each year, but they are in all of the people and things that represent them. We need to go back to work like Demeter and provide for those we love who are here. But it is true the line was drawn in the sand on September 11. It remains to be seen how this event will change us and the world, but it has forever changed us as a people.

So there are cycles in all of our lives. If we really paid attention to our life, we could see the cycles: job changes, body changes, and relationships. Just as the moon and sun come up and set each day, we too have cycles as people, families, and nations. Our nation has experienced one of those momentous times that changed our cycle as a nation—like the myth of Persephone, about life and death, and the effect on mass consciousness. But it is not a myth; it is the truth of our lives. There will be story after story being told about that day, as it has been since the death of President Kennedy. Each one of us knows where we were when it happened. All the stories will be told from all the families, police, and fire fighters. Stories will be told by those near and far and whether we saw it on our TVs or out our windows. The survivor will someday think, "Was this a myth?" because it is the stuff of which myths are made, but this was true. There will be mystical things that cannot be explained that will turn into myth. This event will likely lead to myths for future generations as the stories are told.

When shall we see poets born?
After a time of disasters and great misfortunes,
when harrowed nations begin to breathe again. And then, shaken
by the terror of such spectacles, imaginations will paint things
entirely strange to those who have not witnessed them.
(Denis Diderot)

Dealing with loss and death is the biggest piece of our lives; the other is birth.

For me, this myth held just as much significance as the hope myth. I lost my daughter and wandered hopelessly to find my little Hope. By moving forward to help others, I could go on and feel as if life could be lived once again. Each person I can reach out to gives me back my daughter, Hope.

How do you relate your loss experience to the Persephone myth?

Can you think of a myth or story that relates to loss in your life?

The Tree of Life

A seed hidden in the heart of an apple is an orchard invisible.

(Welsh Proverb)

Hope deferred makes the heart sick, but a desire fulfilled is a tree of life.

(Proverbs 13:12)

I love trees! Christmas trees, willow trees, cottonwood trees, and although I have never seen one, I am sure I could be brought to my knees by a redwood in California. Growing up on a farm in the Midwest, I spent hours in and under trees. I remember being very young and having a fascination with parchment. I think my mother ordered a copy of the Declaration of Independence and was teaching me about how this country started and our liberties. I seemed to be more excited about the look of the "fake" parchment paper than the concepts at that age. My mother told me about the paper and how they sometimes wrote on paper made from bark. I thought parchment was made from bark, and I thought I could make paper from bark. I had a favorite window from which to gaze out and look over our yard into the cornfield. It was from that view I saw what I thought was the tree that the founding fathers must have used to write their important ideals. It was a beautiful white Birch. We had only one. I do believe it was planted alongside an apple and a pear tree. I remember getting a knife from the kitchen drawer, and I headed out to make myself some parchment. I did cut off a piece, as I remember about the size of half sheet of writing paper. I do not remember what I did next, but I do remember the next season seeing that I had killed off one-half of the tree from ripping the bark. I was horrified. I think I even prayed to God to heal that tree. I hated myself for killing it and being so thoughtless, an interesting and good lesson for a child; also interesting is what we remember from childhood and what we don't.

When we moved to town when I was 11, I drew the huge willow tree in the neighbor's yard. It held a kind of spell over me, the branches gracefully bowed and swayed in the breeze. Sitting under it made me feel like a grand lady. To this day, I live close to one of the largest Ponderosa Pine forests in the world and enjoy driving through them as much as possible. When I arrived in Sedona, I would go into one of the canyons and meditate. I searched for a tree that would be my tree to sit in and under. I would take my teacher and friend where we would study and talk about the Kabbalah under this tree.

The Tree of Life appears in all cultures. To the ancient Mayans heaven was on earth but it was hidden from mankind by a mystical mountain. Their Tree of Life was a cross with the center as the beginning; the Source of all life. The branches were the under world, earth and sky. In the Nordic culture the Tree is the spring water of all knowledge. Chinese tell of a peach tree that bares fruit every 3000 years. And the one who eats the peach will have immortal life.

Humans and trees are distant cousins, in that they are made of the same stuff, just as is the entire universe. The difference in tree and human DNA is in the arrangement of the pieces, and in the number of chromosomes.

The Kabbalah or the Tree of Life entered my life one day while teaching. According to Google: "*Kabbalah is the ancient Jewish tradition of mystical interpretation of the Bible, first transmitted orally and using esoteric methods (including ciphers). It reached the height of its influence in the later Middle Ages and remains significant in Hasidism."*

What follows is an experience that led me to the writing of this book. It was years after Hope had been born, and my husband and I were separated. He had succumbed to alcohol and was living actively in his disease. It was a very bad time. I have always believed that he held out and held up our family during those darkest hours after the loss. Now, it was time for him to grieve and fall apart. We felt it best to put him on a bus to home, in Chicago. My son and I found a small apartment and I was now raising a 13-year-old boy on my own. I had gotten a job in a neighboring small town teaching high school. I knew the man who started the school, and by luck, I ran into him at the post office, and he offered me a position. The first year was trying, but the second year is when everything began unraveling for me.

In the spring of that year, I was sent into a regular classroom. I had been teaching the most challenged boys with disabilities, emotional problems, and most had committed a crime and were on probation. These were my kind of kids. But because of infractions done by the school, parents were upset with the administration about how I and the boys were being treated. As with many systems, the misfits are cast out and unattended. I was punished by being ripped out of the program and away from the boys. Behind the scenes, parents and a teacher and friend of mine who had just resigned, were going to meet to take the problems to the state board and higher, perhaps to the attorney general, for possible illegal activity by the school. So I was under tremendous stress.

In the middle of all this, my father was gravely ill and had just recently passed, another loss on top of all the losses I had endured, including the loss of the boys at school. So here is the background that led up to what happened to me next. This particular day my class was unusually unruly. I had had enough. So I let them do their thing. I sat down at a table flanked on either side by one girl and one boy who were not participating in the circus in the room. I had determined I would write a new seating chart. Now unbeknownst to me, at that very hour in a home of one of my past students, they were meeting and had called the state about the school.

I proceeded to drown out the noise and tried to make some order out of the chaos on paper. I can remember it so clearly. It was as if these two students on either side of me and I were in a bubble of focus and calm as I wrote. They were assisting me as to where I should conquer and divide. Then it happened. I got a sharp pain in my head. The boy asked if I was okay and I said I was fine, but I was not. Then I went to write the initials of one of the students, T.J. I made the letter T fine, but then I could not remember how to make a J. The girl on my right could see there was something wrong and asked if she should go get someone. I insisted I was fine.

All the while, there was the roar of a high school classroom with their teacher down in action, I tried to continue. The two students beside me were watching me with heightened concern. I know all three of us thought I was having a stroke. So I put my pen on the paper. I could not write. I could not find the letter J in my head; it was blank, as if I were three-years-old again and did not know how to write. Then, as if in slow motion, or more like an invisible hand took over mine, I wrote a symbol that I had never seen before. This was not a J, and how had it gotten there? It was a shock to both me and the two students. By now they were frightened, but they asked, "What is that?" I told them I had no idea. Then the pain left. I could write again and made a J. My guardian students began to breathe again and told me they were sure glad I had made that J! I then decided I had better call the office and have someone take over the class. I was very shaken.

During the last month of my pregnancy with Hope, I developed toxemia, which means I had high blood pressure. In most cases it goes away after birth, but mine had not. So I was convinced I had had a small stroke. I called my doctor and realized it was her day off. Then I called my teacher friend, which is when I learned they had met and called the state. At this point, I must explain about this teacher friend. She was originally from the Caribbean. Healing and mystical teachings were a part of her upbringing. On top of it, her grandparents lived in Cuba. This grandfather was Jewish, and when she visited him, she was taught the Kabbalah. So when I told her about what had just happened, she told me she thought I probably did have a small stroke. She said to go home and call my doctor and rest. But more than concern for my health was the interest in the symbol I had made instead of the J. As I described it, she said it sounded like a letter from another alphabet. She said, "I am not going to tell you what I think it is, but I will meet you at your home." I signed out and headed for home.

I made it home safely, shaken but feeling fine. I had no more pain and was thinking clearly. I hate and mistrust the medical profession and did not want to go to the emergency room or another doctor but mine. So I just lay down and was awakened by my friend with books in her arms. She asked how I was feeling and then wanted to see what the symbol looked like that I had made in my classroom. I drew it for her and she gasped. She opened a book she had brought with her, and there was the symbol just as I had written it. I cannot remember ever seeing this before in my life.

It was the letter Beth in the Hebrew alphabet. She sat in silence looking at me. I asked, "Well, what does that mean?" She told me she had waited her entire life to receive something like this. And without trying, here I was with no knowledge, training, or heritage link and I had been given a gift. (I later learned that my great, great grandmother was a German Jew who married a Christian man and was cast out of her family.)

What kind of gift was this, a pain in my head and then a strange letter out of nowhere? She began to tell me about what she knew about this letter. In Hebrew, each letter has a number value, and it symbolizes more than just the use in a word. Beth, according to *The Practical Kabbalah Guidebook* by C. J. M. Hopking represents as follows: "The House. Beth is the first letter of the first word in the Bible, *be-Rashith* means 'in the beginning". It is used to represent creation. A house is a container for the household consequently, Binah, the Great Mother, is considered to hold her creation of all of the lower worlds in her womb."

It also means the "mouth" of man. Whatever goes into the body to nourish it, it then sends "the words of life" out through the mouth. The vocal cords and mouth are used and Beth lies there with the mystery of the Word Transcendent. It is also the number 2. I was born on January 2nd.

Beth's key word is Formation. It forms sounds in patterns. Form, as in the formation of a baby in the womb, and as in the feminine principle for humanity.

And a direct quote from Hopking's book about Beth: *"...man's physical body will be lifted beyond the limitations of disease and death. Man and woman will be equal in the world and mankind will know that noble fulfillment of the Song of Solomon, 'The King's Daughter shall be all glorious within'."*

And there was more, much more. My friend then told me she was about to start teaching me about the most sacred of mystical Jewish teachings, the Kabbalah. I was not Jewish, but she said for some reason spirit sent that letter in that place and time for some reason. It would be up to me to discover why.

She spent some months working with me but then told me she would give me some books and some of her notes. I was on my own. In the Kabbalah, you are to be taught orally by a trained instructor. She told me that because of my experience, she did not feel she could teach me anymore and that spirit was teaching me. This was too much for me to hear after all I had been through. Her comment was "I think the experiences that you had and are having are why this has happened. You are having a spiritual breakthrough." So I studied. What I was exposed to could fill another book. But one day, I awoke and heard, "You must write a book about your daughter and Hope." How would I do that? The thought popped into my head; go into nature. I lived in one of the most beautiful places on the planet: Sedona, Arizona. So this was not a chore but a joy. Sedona itself holds much power.

I would go out on the land as much as I could and meditate. Some days it was peaceful and calm, and at other times, the thoughts would pour into me about what to write. I would dream what to write and where to get clues on what to write. The process was an awesome experience in itself. All the while I was living through another stressful and unhappy time in my life with the school business. But the studying of the Kabbalah and the preparations to write kept me going. Finally, at the end of the school year, I decided I could no longer deal with the stress and resigned. I had no new job on the horizon. I just knew all would be well and I needed to study and write. I was on unemployment for over six months, and I immersed myself in the process of my new life and the book.

There is an old Hebrew legend that tells of a Rabbi that gave Adam the secrets of the Kabbalah and of alchemy. The Rabbi promised when mankind understood these mysteries the curse of the forbidden fruit from the tree of knowledge would be lifted and humans could once again enter the garden.

In the middle ages, the Tree of Life became a popular name for the Kabbalah. As with many things in our modern world, we do not know where many of the thoughts or languages originated without study. It is also what Jacob saw when he had the dream of the ladder. Jacob's ladder is a reference from the Bible's Old Testament, Genesis 28:10-22. Jacob has a dream about a stairway resting on the Earth, with its top reaching to Heaven, and the angels of God were ascending and descending on it.

And he dreamed,
And behold a ladder set up on the Earth,
And the top of it reached to Heaven:
And behold the angels of God ascending and descending on it.

(King James Version)

In the Kabbalists' thought, this dream was a symbolic vision of alchemic powers. It was a rainbow ladder with red and blue being the main colors. Red was thought to be "spirit", and blue was "matter". Since the discovery of the DNA strand, it could mean just that: spirit into matter. Could it be Jacob was given the information for Kabbalah, through his DNA, in a dream? Our DNA is in the shape of a spiraling ladder. Also could that be why the Kabbalah was supposed to stay with the heritage of the Hebrew people? I had it in me from my great-great-great grandmother.

In tradition of the Kabbalah, it is believed that all humans must climb the ladder, or tree, so to speak. All of us are at the bottom, and we have the opportunity to make our way up the tree through certain emanations and fields. We must go through lower thoughts and emotions, and then pass through the field of Hope to get to Beauty, which represents the true nature of the Self. From this point, there are the higher concepts, and finally, the highest of spiritual realms; it leads us to move up into the highest areas of spirit. This is what I believe to be our spiral shaped DNA: Jacob's ladder and/or the Tree of Life.

This all happened amidst a separation from my husband and feeling great loss that I may never have him back. It was a very scary and intense time. However, those thoughts diminished in view of what I was writing about, what I knew to be the truth, that there is everlasting Hope, no matter what. My husband lived and came home to us!

Could the circumstances in my life, the death of my child, and my marital discord, cause me to surface a bit of information from this strand to my conscious mind? Could it have been these losses and stresses that caused a message from deep inside myself to set me on course, on the course I am on today? Sometimes it takes trauma in the form of a perceived loss to turn us to a new focus. It is my intent to help us to know that we are good and that there is always, in matter, somewhere to turn. This is the place we can bring ourselves back to life and love and joy. It is our God-given gift!

I love how the universe works when we are on the right track; the synchronicities flow like water. Right after I wrote the previous paragraphs, I read the following:

> *It's not until the unexpected loss of those they love that they're reminded of just how precious their family, and their time together, really is. For the survivors, "LOSS" becomes the catalyst that awakens them from one way of looking at life and jolts them into new perceptions.*
>
> (Gregg Braden)

And so it goes, that when we are pushed to what we perceive is the end of our rope, then we see things in a new light and turn toward wanting the answers that ultimately literally live inside of us. I believe that Hope is neither a feeling nor just a thought concept, it is a part of the matter of our bodies in our DNA.

Rather than being your thoughts and emotions, be the awareness behind them.
(Eckhart Tolle)

Part IV

Thought As Matter; Our Mind

Thought As Matter

What is the matter?

When something is <u>not</u> going well we hear others ask this question.

We know what that question means but I wanted to look at it in a deeper sense. What does *matter* mean? I found it very interesting that it has a very scientific meaning and then some curious other meanings. The first thing I see in the dictionary is: **material, stuff, wood**...I thought WOOD? Wood (derived from the base of mater, MOTHER), originally the growing of the trunk of a tree. HM! So I looked up mater, sure enough mother, often preceded by THE. (Just a stream of conscience thought for a moment.) Mate is an evergreen tree in South America, and did you know the first meaning for Matrix is THE WOMB?

Back to Matter...

...what a thing is made of, what ALL things are made of, whatever occupies space and is perceptible to the senses in some way.

In Physics matter and energy are regarded as equivalents, mutually convertible according to Einstein's formula $E = mc^2$. Atoms are the basic building blocks of matter and that includes our bodies. The Einstein formula really makes the case for the fact that matter is just light or energy in a confined space. This means that ALL matter is alive.

The old thought, before Einstein, separated the mind and matter. The old model of the universe did not connect the pieces of the universe together. It was like a machine with no interchangeable parts. We now know we are all connected and made of the same stuff. We will get back to this later on these pages.

The next definition of Matter means: **an important affair, a moment, and an unfavorable state of affairs; trouble, difficulty.**

Materialism is another definition, the doctrine that matter is the only reality and that everything in the world, including thought, will, and feeling, can be explained only in terms of matter (in contrast to idealism). But many scientists will tell you that thought is matter. After all, light and sound have matter, so why not thought?

"What is the matter?" In almost all of these cases when someone asks that question, the one definition is that of the **unfavorable affair.**

I find it interesting that there are two meanings for 'matter' that correspond, one with the other, and this is the point of the entire workbook. When we hear the above statement it always means that someone outside (or we, inside ourselves) observes there is a problem, an unfavorable affair. From this unfavorable affair there is a thought or feeling that is giving us pain. Despair and hopelessness comes from such a place. Have you not heard this question when someone is in pain? When examining the question, what are your thoughts? Does it mean I feel sick, I feel sad, I don't have enough money this month, my father died or I feel lonely?

Now take a look at the definition of matter on a pure scientific level, thought as 'matter'. In many cases of 'matter" we feel as if we are powerful enough to change the form of it. Cooking, drawing, mowing the lawn, planting gardens and giving birth, anything we do in life has to do with the manipulation of matter. We have developed TV, radio, computers, lasers, all which stem from waves of energy and sources from the earth and universe. These last examples of matter are closer to what I am referring to when I talk about thought. If we can harness the radio waves then we can harness thought waves.

So let's now ponder thoughts as matter. Thought is vibration. Vibration is evidence of energy. Energy is the power that creates, maintains, or destroys, depending upon the intensity and quality of the force producing it.

From Love, Medicine and Miracles by Bernie Siegel, *"I feel that all disease is ultimately related to lack of love, or to love that is only conditional love, for the exhaustion and depression of the immune system thus created leads to physical vulnerability. I also feel that all healing is related to the ability to give and accept unconditional love."*

He goes on to say, *"One of the immediate rewards is a live message to the body. I am convinced that unconditional love is the most powerful known stimulant of the immune system. If I told patients to raise their blood levels of immune globulins or killer T cells, no one would know how. But if I can teach them to love themselves and others fully, the same changes happen automatically. The truth is: love heals."*

As Dr. Seigel tells us, he believes that everything stems from lack of love. I agree, but I also say it stems from thinking negative thoughts. "I feel sick, I feel sad, I can't do this, I can't manage my life"…on and on.

So, if thought is matter, and it becomes "an unfavorable" matter, that "thought matter" can make us emotional and physically ill, just as spoiled food or bad water can make us sick. FOOD FOR THOUGHT! Thought is food for our minds and soul. What we think makes things happen. We either can be creative, healthy, and happy or sick, and sad.

The world as we have created it is a process of our thinking. It cannot be changed without changing our thinking.
(Albert Einstein)

Positive thoughts can attract what you need and want. And the negative ones bring only negative outcomes.

There is a science that started in the 1960's with the name of Psychotronics. Psyche in Greek means "breath or spirit" and -tron means "instrument"" The science is based on the concept that a psychotron is a wave length that is thought. It is instantaneous and travels faster than light. The U.S. Psychotronics Organization states: *"Man and all life forms share a common ground in that they are submerged in the electromagnetic field of the earth. Each life form, in turn, has its own electromagnetic field, and distortions of these fields are the cause of diseases in organisms. It follows, then, in their line of thought, that correcting the energy distortions should enable healing."*

In *Energy, Matter and Form*, Christopher Hills and his associates talk about experiments done with psychotronics: *"These (experiments with thoughts) indicate the presence of stronger attractive force than magnetic, possibly a bio-gravitational force. It becomes 'lower' forms of energy and even 'matter' by following the laws of transformation. That is, it gradually slows down the rate of vibration as it meets other waves, in the same way that gas, steam, changes to liquid, water, and to solid, ice as the temperature decreases."*

Our universe is based on electromagnetic energy. Our bodies are no different. Our bodies resonate at a level of 0.1 to 30Hz in the brain. This is the electromagnetic brain wave. The earth has an electromagnetic resonance as well. It measures at 7.5Hz to 30Hz. The brain vibrates at different levels at different activities. Sleeping is 0.5-35Hz, head pain is 13-30Hz. Intense mental concentration is 14-30Hz. We are in a sense an electromagnetic generator.

So you see, what our thoughts do is change our energy (matter or the outcome in matter). Our brain controls the energy but our mind controls and creates the thoughts and images to direct that energy. We can create matter by our thoughts.

Matter is a string of molecules strung together. Our thoughts are chains of thoughts strung together to create an outcome. For example:

If you are thinking about the fact that you really love your dad and you want to bake him a cake for his birthday, you can walk through the entire experience in your mind and see it in your mind's eye first: going to the store, making the cake, decorating it with candles, feeling the excitement of dad's response and finally a party for dad. Everyone eats cake and you have created love and sweet nourishment for family and friend. You thought it and dreamed it. Now you go out make it happen. The mind is a wonderful and powerful tool.

Positive self talk is thinking of positive words and phrases you can say to yourself. When you find you are doing the negative, gently tell your old self to change to something that feels better. Depression can turn to expression, talk it out, create by writing, drawing, singing etc.

Egoism can turn to confidence.

Extravagance into simplicity.

Hate to love.

And on and on. You must have the desire to want to change first and know that "stinkin' thinkin'" creates nothing but destructive results.

Our personalities can be seen as the effects of subtle thought patterns in the medium of our actions. Even though the mind may not be matter in the sense that a brick is, it is a vibrational form, a subtler and more elusive form. This is what makes working with the mind such a difficult craft—it's slippery and elusive substance is difficult to capture and mold into a design in tune with nature.
....there is no world of external matter, that what we see are interference patterns created within our own vibrating consciousness.
(Christopher Hills, Phil Allen, Alastair Bearne, Roger Smith)

The Free Dictionary.com defines matter: "to be of importance." The matter of our Hope was of importance for sure to us but she is and was of more importance than to us as parents. She mattered just as you matter. We all matter. The new movement in the black community because of all the killings says as their slogan; Black Lives Matter. We all matter; Humanity Matters and all Life

Matters. No matter if you live 5 minutes or 100 years the spirit has come to this earth for a reason and that does matter. Know YOU in this moment and always matter.

"You matter. You are important. There is a reason for your existence. You may not see or understand how this is true, but truth doesn't cease to be truth because of doubt, blindness, or ignorance. And the truth is—
you matter."

(Richelle E. Goodrich)

What Were You Thinking?!

As you take pause to read the question above, what were you thinking at the time?

Being aware of what thoughts are in our heads is a challenge. It seems as if we are taught that thoughts just are in our minds. However, we do have control over those thoughts and in turn having this awareness can change our lives.

Your brain shall be your servant instead of your master,
You will rule it instead
of allowing it to rule you.

(Charles E. Popplestone)

WHAT ARE YOU THINKING…NOW?

Find time in your day to stop and check your thoughts. At first it will have to be almost scheduled but as time goes on you will check often and eventually know what is going on in your head most of the time.

Upon rising be aware of your thoughts. Do you want to change them to set the tone for the day?

If you have a break in the morning, check your thoughts.

When you are eating, check your thoughts.

Before you go to bed, check your thoughts.

If you never change your mind, why have one?

(Edward De Bono)

Negative to Positive Thoughts

If your mind is empty, it is always
Ready for anything;
It is open to everything.
In the beginner's mind there are many possibilities;
In the expert's mind there are few.

(Shunryu Suzuki-roshi)

Let us look at our thoughts. I must say at this point this is not about feelings, it is about thoughts.

Feelings are not negative or positive; they are emotions, and there is no judgment.

Remember grief is not negative. Grief is a natural course of loss but there comes a time to move on. If you find yourself not able to move on these exercises may help. Sometimes we can feel guilty about being happy after loss but as I said in the beginning of the book, you do deserve to be happy again. If you are in the early stages of grief you might want to just read over this or even come back to this later.

EXERCISE:

What phrase do you repeat over and over again in your head or out loud that is negative?
Example:
I will never get over this pain of losing my loved one! Or, I will never get well. There is no hope for me.

Write down one of the phrases that you repeat to yourself.

Now change that around to becoming a positive statement ... even if you do not believe it right now. (I will feel happy again someday, or I am well, or there is hope for me.)

Now say it over to yourself 7 times. How does that feel?

It may feel uncomfortable at first because you may not feel as if you really mean it. For now, what is important is the act of changing the thoughts from negative to positive.

Practice this over the next several days. You will be changing a pattern. Try to become aware of any negative thought. When you catch yourself thinking a negative thought, look at the negative thought and try to think about what feeling is attached it.

Next, change the negative to what you really want to happen in the positive.
Example:
Negative –I will never get over this pain of loss. (feeling hopeless and unworthy)

Positive—I will be happy again and still remembering my loved one. I will have hope for my life. Or even better—I am happy and I am remembering my loved one with joy. I have hope for my life.

As with anything new we are learning we must repeat and repeat over and over until it becomes second nature. Changing patterns are not easy. If we have been taught as child to think negative it may take more time to change but if the desire is there we can change anything.

Awareness is the Key!

Keep up the pattern and write down in a journal how you feel as you change the pattern.

Then write down the changes, things, and events that happen around you as you change the thought patterns.

If something you want is slow to come to you, it can be for only one reason: You are spending more time focused upon its absence than you are about its presence.
(Esther Hicks)

Conscious Living

As you start to walk out on the way, the way appears.

(Rumi)

Life is a series of steps, one step at a time. If we live consciously it is like walking in the sand, we are able to see each step. When we are aware of each step and see it we then know where to place the next. We will be lead to where we want to go by being aware of each and every step as we are walking. We must not look behind at our steps; they have already been swept away by the winds of time. If we do look back we lose our awareness of where we are walking in the moment, many steps are lost and we can lose our way.

To live consciously is to become aware in the moment of where we are going, noting each and every movement as we do it. Thinking not of the past or looking at the path in front of us but just the one step in that moment. It is awareness, 100% aware of where we are at each step of the way.

We need to live in a way that frees us. Having any attachment to anything limits us. Being detached allows us to live our life without burdens, without constant thought of these things and people, it frees our minds and hearts to be open and ready for what is coming our way. There is no loss. There is no loss because there is nothing to lose. It was never yours to begin with. You are all there is in this moment. And it is all you.

We should not be attached because we are not separated. Attachment means you see yourself separate. The truth is we are not separate. We are all one!

To live consciously is see beauty all around you. Notice nature or people's smiles or art and music. To live allowing beautiful things to affect you, you then become a sponge soaked in grace. People will feel this in you and may even say to you how great you look or that you seem so happy.

Do not think of beauty as something separate from you; make it a part of everyday life. Driving to work notice the sky every morning. Make it a habit. Make it a part of living with awareness. Become aware of beauty everywhere.

If you are not taking responsibility for your state of consciousness, you are not taking responsibility for life.
(Eckhart Tolle)

Conscious living means awareness. When someone speaks to you, really listen. Not just to their words but listen with your eyes, with all your senses. Notice their body language and the tone of their voice. There should be no attachment to what you will say back. Leave yourself out of it. Just listen.

Think consciously. As I wrote about thoughts we can create our lives by how we think. So start by tossing out the random thoughts that bring negative responses. Consciously monitor them. If they are coming from an emotion, acknowledge it and feel those feelings, but never hang on to them to avoid those feelings. Think about where you are now. Be here in the moment and what comes your way deal with it and keep moving, being aware.

Begin to live each moment in awareness. Don't think about what is next. Be into what is happening in your life right now and act accordingly. Living in this way you will look up and simply feel hope. You will see her in someone else's eyes as you listen, you will see it in a sunset, smell it as you pass a bakery baking fresh bread, or even in someone's voice telling how sorry they are for your loss. Yes, even in the midst of things going in a way we did not expect if we begin to live consciously hope arrives on your doorstep.

Like attracts like. Whatever the conscious mind thinks and believes, the subconscious identically creates.

(Brian Adams)

Write down what living consciously would be like at this point in your life. Sometimes we need to imagine what it would be like so then in daily life we have a road map.

Brain Gym

These exercises were created and developed by Dennison & Dennison. In keeping with the authors' wishes, I would like to acknowledge all rights and mention given to Edu-Kinesthetics Publications.

All of these exercises are simple and fun movements that enhance whole brain learning. The word education comes from the Latin word *educare*, which means "to draw out." Kinesiology derived from the Greek root Kinesis, means "motion" and is the study of the movement of the human body.

For our purposes, we will be doing self-concept, memory & abstract thinking, and creative thinking exercises.

Self-Concept

Self-esteem is both the goal and means of self-directed learning.

Having confidence with the boundaries of personal space helps one to feel safe, to know when risk-taking is appropriate, and to respect other people's space. Personal space is the immediate working area around the body, including all the space one can comfortably reach in any direction. Into this space one radiates thoughts, feelings, and self-expression.

Positive Points

Think of something you would like to remember. Close your eyes and allow yourself to experience the image or to experience the associated tension and then release.

- Sit in a comfortable position. Lightly touch the point above each eye with the fingertips of each hand. The points are halfway between the hairline and the eyebrows.

This may be done with a partner to allow more relaxation.

These points are the neurovascular balance points for the stomach meridian. People tend to hold stress in the abdomen, resulting in stomachaches and nervous stomachs, a pattern that may start in childhood. This exercise can help blood flow from the hypothalamus to the frontal lobes, where rational thoughts occur. This prevents the fight-or-flight response, so new responses can be learned.

Hook-up

Hook-ups connect the electrical circuits in the body, containing and thus focusing both attention and disorganized energy. The mind and body relax as energy circulates through areas blocked by tension. The touching of the fingertips balances and connects the two brain hemispheres.

- Sit in a comfortable position and cross left ankle over the right.
- Extend arms before you, crossing the left wrist over the right.
- Now interlace your fingers and draw your hands up toward your chest.
- Close your eyes, breathe deeply, and relax for about one minute.

- After the minute, uncross your legs. Undo your fingers and now touch the fingertips of both hands together, while breathing deeply for one more minute.

This exercise can help you listen better, improve self-control, and increase comfort in an environment. It helps to balance the left and right brain. Excessive energy to the brain can manifest as depression, pain, fatigue, or hyperactivity.

Meditation is the dissolution of thoughts in Eternal awareness or Pure consciousness without objectification, knowing without thinking, merging finitude in infinity.
(Voltaire)

Be In This World But Not of It.

This is a tricky thing. To be here and yet we are to never let go of the fact that we are "souls with bodies not bodies with souls". We come from the spiritual realm and leave to go to that place when we leave this world. But this thing called "life" is in-between with all of the games, toys, and distractions. How are we to be in this world but not of it?

What we call the personality has our ego attached to it. Our personality loves and hates things on the planet. We have illusions and barriers that soon keep us away from our soul or spiritual connections. In order, to not be attached to the ego or the material plane we need to be totally present.

We tend to shut down who we truly are as spirit and as a result we shut out the light and our own consciousness. If we live true and honest with little thought and little attachment to people, places, and things we can begin to live here…now in this life yet connected to spiritual plane all the time. Be Present!

(Taken from "Conscious Living Newsletter" by Alice Molter-Serrano)

Part V

Spirit As Matter

Sound into Matter

In the beginning was the Word, and the Word was with God was the word.

(Bible, New International Version)

If we are to believe what the Bible tells us it means that vibration was before any matter. It states that vibration formed matter. It is the "mater" of all things. So everything you see around you is a frequency. The more the frequency changes and vibrates to a higher level the more "things" in matter change.

All Matter in the Universe is Sound
All matter originates and exists only by virtue of a force...We must assume behind this force the existence of a conscious and intelligent Mind. This Mind is the matrix of all matter.

(Max Planck)

Sound turns matter and energy into form.

(David Icke)

So if the "conscious mind" that spoke and made all things, we too, in the image of this force can make things change into matter with the sounds of our thought, of our words, or music.

Sound is a vibration; an explosion disturbs the place where the vibration is concentrated, it affects the earth and the atmosphere for great distances. On 9/11/01, not only did the planes hitting the towers affect us, but the vibration of that hit can be felt in our bodies as well. It was not just a spiritual, emotional and physical distribution but also on a vibration level that all persons around the area could feel. When you hear people ask, "What was the worst part of the experience?" some would say, "The sound of the building coming down was unbelievable." This vibration will live in those survivors for years to come. And I wonder how it did affect them on a physical level.

Let us change or even create new things in matter by the sounds of our voices, the sounds of our lives. No more negative self talk or speaking out loud of other negative ideas. Placing them out into the world we then create what we do not want.

Sound is a vibration.
Brian Greene tells us: *"Well, all sounds—all music in particular—comes from vibrations. So the reason why you can hear me speak is because I am creating pressure waves that are emanating from my mouth, compressing the air, then rarifies as it spreads out, and compresses again. And that ripple of air ultimately bangs into your eardrum, smashes your eardrum with these molecules of air, going back and forth and your eardrum registers and your brain decodes that. And you have the sensation of hearing. So all sound is a matter of producing those pressure waves, those vibrations in air."*

Music
Music can help us heal. If your thoughts are too much to deal with, listen to music that uplifts you. Just like our thought the vibration can cause a negative or positive response. Music enhances unconscious receptivity to symbolism. It can generate a sense of safety and well-being. Music can

boost productivity and can change our perception of space and time. Music can change our thoughts and elevate our spirit.

Before moving to the next section; listen to The Marriage of Figaro by Mozart.

Or Dance #12 from the Twelve German Dances, K. 586 by Mozart.

Or Any Mozart.

Also, if you can get a recording of Gregorian Chants or any type of chanting.

200 years after Mozart's birth, French physician, Dr. Alfred Tomatis, researched the link between how children learn and their sonic environment. Tomatis discovered that a person hears even before birth and that this pre-natal auditory experience is a critical facet of early childhood development. His research has further shown that for people with learning disabilities and other developmental disorders, Mozart's music can provide an audio "bridge" of sorts, allowing many people to overcome previously impassable developmental blocks.

(Don Campbell)

Spirit in Matter

Spirit and matter are the two names of life. The primal aspect of life developing into denseness remains spirit, and its development into dense form is called matter. It is like water turning into snow, it is liquid, but it develops into a harder substance, it loses its fineness.

(Hazrat Inayat Khan)

We are spirit in matter. This world makes us think the opposite of the fact, that first we must have form, then spirit, and then we can have matter. Spirit in matter is life, consciousness walking.

To most of us this symbol means to add. And this is true; however, I understand why this symbol is used for addition. If the vertical line is spirit and the horizontal line is matter then we have something and something added to something brings abundance. It means to add to it. It really symbolizes the coming of the spirit into the womb of the mother.

What we call matter is consciousness itself.

(www.scienceandnonduality.com)

Spirit does live without matter, but matter does not exist without spirit. The woman can live without the child but a child cannot live without a mother. The soul comes to the earth to learn and live. This life, as I see it, is a classroom and every single thing we learn while in the matter of the body progresses, the soul and spirit of the human. Spiritual energy cannot be destroyed. We now know through science what the holy men knew from the beginning of time that our energy, our spirit never dies. That means we live on after the matter of our body has become old and worn out. The spirit lives on.

The everlasting light and love of the other world, the spiritual world, is within us no matter what we believe. It is a part of everything in matter. The cross represents this world with all the things of the flesh and the five senses. Spirit guiding it all.

Michael Berg tells us: "*The kabbalists teach that what is called the Endless Light is in everything. When you are enjoying a steak, for example, whatever joy you extract from eating the steak is the same joy you can experience from looking at, let's say, a chair, because the Endless Light is in that as much as it is in the steak. But it all has to do with your spiritual sense, your sense of smell. Every time we act in the way of Desire to Receive for the Self Alone, we corrupt our senses even more, and we need more of the external things to excite us, to make us happy.*"

We are not of this world. We are of the spiritual world. We come into this place, this material world to progress our own soul. We must keep our eyes on the light and even though we are given amnesia upon entering this world we need to wake up to this fact we are spirit not the body. Matter of our body is a gift to express the negative and positive so we can be all we are meant to be. We are never finished. There is more to learn. If you can see this material world from a distance, a detached perspective, we can understand and see clearer. You have the spiritual part of you that looks out for you. This higher self is what we all need to stay connected to. When making decisions and watching how the world works stand back and do not take it personally. Our body is the vehicle and through it we stay fixed to this world. And messages come to us through it. But as my acupuncturist, Sig, says, "don't take your body personally." Within our body is memory of all higher concepts, not just Hope but Compassion, Courage, Mercy and all of them. It is through the body that all of these can be expressed.

Thomas Blount writes, "*Every flower of the field, every fiber of a plant, every particle of an insect, and carries with it the impress of its Maker, and can—if duly considered—read us lectures of ethics or divinity.*"

But there are so many other spirits on this planet. There are the spirits of animals and nature. All are equal to the human spirit. All of this planet and those who inhabit it are spirits in matter. Our earthly reality is all about that. Without spirit nothing is alive. As a modern society so many of us forget that the planet itself is filled with spirit. The earth is alive with earthquakes, volcanoes and weather. This is life and energy. We have become so myopic in our ideas of what spirit can be that we do not recognize the other spirits of the planet. The aborigines of any region will tell you about the spirit of the rocks, of the animals and even of the sky. Everything that is alive is spirit and it is that when we are unaware of this very fact we are out of balance.

Without the Matter of Hope or the knowledge that there is hope we become the walking dead. We are in the matter of the body, not using our spirit as a learning tool. Without the thoughts, the emotions, the sounds, and the eyes of hope do we realize what life is all about? We live, we learn, we transform, we slip into the other world and live on forever.

There is a conflict between spirit and matter. The matter absorbs the spirit in order to exist, and the spirit assimilates matter, for it is its own property. The whole of manifestation may thus be regarded as continual conflict between spirit and matter; the spirit developing into matter on the one hand and spirit assimilating matter on the other; the former being called activity and the latter silence, or construction and destruction, or life and death. When one realizes that the source of both spirit and matter is life, then one will see that there is no such thing as death; but this one can only recognize when knows the distinction between the life which may be called the source and the life which is momentary, the life which matter shows by absorbing spirit.
(Hazrat Inayat Khan)

Meditation as Vibration

A mantra is primarily a mental sound, as the words or sounds we hear are first conceived and energized by the concentrative faculty of the mind and then represented audibly via the larynx and voice box. The only real differences between the physical sound form and the mental thought form are wavelength, frequency and medium. The physical sound is a transformation of a pattern codified in mental wavelengths and frequencies into slower frequencies and longer wavelength of sound.

Mantras are tools for deprogramming and reprogramming our mental computer.

Please do the following meditation.

This is a meditation practiced over 2,500 year ago by Buddhist monks. It will calm your life and keep you connected to your heart.

- Sit in a comfortable fashion. Relax your body.
- Let your mind be quiet, letting go of all plans and activities.
- Then begin to recite inwardly the phrases.
- You may want to visualize yourself as you were as young child, happy and full of loving kindness

---

May I be filled with loving kindness.

May I be well. May I be peaceful and at ease.
May I be happy.

Practice this meditation repeatedly for a number of weeks until the sense of loving-kindness for yourself grows.

When you find yourself in a difficult situation and it begins to take you over remember this meditation (or any other). The great part about meditation is that it is being done in the mind. You can use it anytime and anyplace to help center yourself.

We are great creators and with our thoughts we create our being and life.

Jesus said, *"Ask and ye shall receive."* (Bible)

Faith

The secret of making something work in your lives is, first of all, the deep desire to make it work: then the FAITH and BELIEF that it can work:
Then to hold that clear definite vision in your consciousness and see it working out step by step…..without one thought of doubt or disbelief.

(Eileen Caddy)

Hope and Love

Another story is that Pandora was sent in good faith by Jupiter to bless man, that she was furnished with a box containing her marriage presents, into which every god had put some blessing. She opened the box incautiously, and the blessings all escaped, with the exception of hope. This story seems more probable than the former; for how could hope, so precious a jewel as it is, have been kept in a jar full of all manner of evils, as in the former statement?

It seems no matter what myth you look at, **hope** is in the presence of, or preceded by, FAITH. Faith, Hope, and Love seem to be forever linked. Note love is at the end of the list. For it is through faith and hope that we come to love.

Remember, sometimes we put our faith in something or someone who is not truth for us. In other words, we can not have true faith in something that is harmful, a lie, or destructive. It may take awhile to really understand that we have put our faith in something that is not positive for us.

Ask yourself, "Am I growing from putting faith into this person or thing?"

"Have I become more my true self and can I love unconditionally all people including myself because of this faith?"

"Does this faith benefit me and the world?"

If the answer is no, it is time to let it go and search for true faith.

Have you let a dream or hope for the future drop?
Have you missed seeing or being with some loved one because your faith in them has gone?
Have you become angry with your Higher Power and the Universe for your suffering?

Positive thought produces positive results!

In what does your true faith lie?

Do you have faith in any of the following? List them according to the most faith to the least faith, number 1 being the most and number 10 being the least. Let me start by saying, ranking our faith is not a thing I like to do, it feels a little disrespectful of the concept; however, it gives us a beginning point.

Family
Friends
Religion
Love
Marriage
Doctors
The law
A dream for the future
The universe
Education
God
Self
More?

Take some time to renew your commitment to be faithful to some items you have listed.

Now, complete the following written commitment:

I, _____, renew my faith commitment to _____ and _____ .

In doing so I have placed focus on my love & trust, and I will daily acknowledge this commitment to faith.

Without faith in something you can not have Hope.

Albert Schweitzer once said, "*Faithfulness is the inner power of life which enables us to understand ourselves. As you observe other people, you will see how few of them are faithful. And, yet, as we look at the few who are, it makes us yearn to become more faithful as they are.*"

For your faithful love endures forever.

(Psalms 136)

Synchronicities

**Synchronicities are unusual, unexpected,
not constructed by the human ego.**

(David Richo, Ph.D.)

You will begin to see synchronicities as you feel more Hope. Try not to discount these happenings. You are actually awakening. This is real.

In Greek the word means two words: "joined with" and ""time."

SYNCHRONICITIES:

> The coincidence in time of two or more casually unrelated events which have the same meaning....his implication is clear—certain events in the universe cluster together into meaningful patterns without recourse to the normal pushes and pulls of causality. These synchronicities, therefore, must transcend the normal laws of science, for they are the expression of much deeper movements that originate in the ground of the universe and involve, in an inseparable way, both matter and memory.
>
> (F. David Peat on Carl Jung)

When you begin to first see the synchronicities, hold onto them tightly. Remember them! They help give you faith. Then as you grow and practice, there will be more, and soon, they will become what you are living. There really are no synchronicities any longer, only that you are finally lined up with what is "The Real You" and what is waiting for you created by your own thoughts, hopes, dreams, and the divine. In other words, synchronicities are answers to your questions and hopes in the physical world that you walk into as you are on your path. It is life as a living, breathing spiritual being!

Synchronistic events offer us perceptions that may be useful in our psychological and spiritual growth and may reveal to us, through intuitive knowledge, that our lives have meaning.

(Jean Shinado Bolen, M.D.)

Summing up the entire book, *The Matter of Hope*, with synchronicities is the point. Science has also looked into this subject, and it has everything to do with matter and the mind. How is it that events, or things, show up parallel to thoughts and/or feeling? Do WE manifest these, or does the Universe, OR as some say, it is what the name suggests: that synchronistic event of them both. Is there a new way of looking at ourselves and the Universe, outside anything that has been known before, even outside quantum physics?

As you will find, these moments tend to be creative breakthroughs and/or peak experiences. In some ways, I feel it could be ourselves meeting ourselves when we are totally attuned. I have had many while writing *The Matter of Hope*, and when these occurred I felt as if I were on the right track. It is not science, but it was as if spirits of higher power were giving me messages, "You are doing great; keep it up."

There are so many possibilities, and herein lies the answer…

...with infinite possibilities, how could there be hopelessness...it is physical, scientific proof in matter there are unlimited doors to open, and behind each one is HOPE!

Now: **WARNING! Be prepared to be surprised and delighted!**

Think back over your life and when did you see SYNCHRONICITIES? What was happening at that time? What and why do you think they happened for you? Why were you aware of them?

Natural Course of Life

By law of periodical repetition, everything which has happened once must happen again and again and not capriciously, but at regular periods, and each thing is its own period, not another's each obeying its own law.

(Mark Twain)

The moon and nature, religion and humankind tell us there is a natural course to life. As my circular symbol represents, life is one large circle or cycle. It is not always necessary to understand that natural course; it is something that just is and we accept the fact that there is a cycle. We do know there is gravity but have yet to truly understand it. Gravity is a natural law; it just is. There are also laws that can be called Mystic Laws. These are of the spiritual nature.

The Christian Bible speaks of "a time for everything." There is "A time to live, a time to die." In the Buddhist religion there is what they call The Ten Worlds. These are conditions of living on the planet. The first, I find interesting, it is HELL. It is the state of suffering and despair. They say we find ourselves unable to be free to take any action in this state. The last of the ten is HEAVEN where we are filled with joy, but only for the moment. No matter what your belief there are certain stages, conditions or cycles we all must go through on a spiritual level.

Learning to deal with these "natural laws of life" for us are like when we were kids and finding out that in order to live we must sleep, eat and rid ourselves of waste. Children have to learn to care for their health and bodies, it is a natural law. So it is as we grow older, there are other natural laws we must learn to deal with.

When you look down on a spiral you will see a circle. You move away from it and it does not look like it a circle at all. Our perception tells us it is a multi-level, multi-dimensional figure. Spirals move around in circle at 360 degrees. The movement in the different dimensions creates growth. A spiral is a living circle and it is our DNA. It is the cycle of man.

Are you going in circles or spirals of growth? What cycles are you dealing with in your life?

How do you feel about dealing with this cycle?

What have you done to help yourself through this cycle?

The Stillness That Is You

Death is a stripping away of all that is not you.
The secret of life is to "die before you die"—and find that there is no death.

(Eckhart Tolle)

Be still. Become Silent. After all that I have written there is more, much more. It is beyond thought. Beyond emotion, and far past, beyond all we think we know. Now we must take a bigger step into finding hope once and for all.

We all have attachments. This is the third dimension and the world after all. We have great attraction to where we live. We care about our home town, our dwelling, and the everyday people in our lives. We become attached to beloved objects; photos of family and friends, a chair that great aunt gave us or our desk and computer. We believe they are a part of us and our lives depend upon on them. In reality they have nothing to do with our true self. They are a part of what Eckhart Tolle says is the "mind created self". The mind is where our ego resides. It is the left hemisphere of our brain. It is where math, science, and reasoning come from. The right hemisphere houses our creativity, music, and sense of space and wonder.

Dr. Jill Bolte Taylor was a brain scientist until one day she had a stroke. This stroke took out the entire left hemisphere of her brain. In her book, *Stroke of Insight*, she talks about how as it was happening she was like an observer. She knew she was losing the concepts of everything around her. No longer did she know names for objects and numbers, and words meant nothing. But she would stop and sense the water in the shower feeling absolutely wonderful and get lost in the process. She was having moments of elation. But there were moments when the left side of her brain kicked in and told her "We are having trouble. Get some help." While in the hospital she noticed there were two kinds of people, those who gave her energy and those who took it. The right hemisphere was all she had left. She knew energy and how things felt. When her mother came to see her, she had no idea who this person was. But when she got in bed with her and began to hold her like a baby, she said, "I like this feeling and this person." Jill had to relearn everything about the left brain once she had surgery. She tells us that when she got home she would sit on the couch and not be able to feed herself, do her hair, or brush her teeth but she would sit and smile feeling totally at peace.

Years later she had to make a decision to relearn things from her old life, which she had NO memory of, or to go on living, becoming a new Jill. She liked the way she was feeling and said she did not want to revisit the old self and went through a period of grief of the knowledge of the loss of that person. Literally, Jill "died before she died" as Eckhart Tolle states, and she lived on as a new person. She writes that one of the biggest things she learned was how we must all be responsible for the energy we give out to other people. Do we take energy or give it? Do we live mostly in our left brain of reason and thought, or do we live through our right brain where we feel and share love?

Attachments are a part of the left brain. The biggest attachments we have are our loved ones and our ego. Attachments are not loving but loving is not attachments, either. The place, the space where true love exists, is not where emotions are, nor is it thought; it is just love.

It's human nature to get attached when we've invested a lot of time in something. But an investment is only as valuable as its return—meaning, we owe it to ourselves to recognize when we can get a better one by wiping the slate clean and starting over.
(Lori Deschene)

My brother died of cancer at the age of 27, and I was only 19. He was the light of my life. Like all little sisters, I looked up to him. He took care of me when he was a teenager because both parents had to work, and I even went on dates with his girlfriend and wife to be. I loved him deeply.

Three days after his death I was having a nightmare. I felt a hand on my hand which woke me up. I opened my eyes thinking I was going to see my mother, but to my astonishment, I saw an outline of what I thought was a ghost. I quickly noticed it was my brother. He had touched my hand to wake me from my misery, and there he stood for only a few seconds. But what happened next is why I am writing about this experience. When his human form disappeared, the room was full of love. It was so palpable that you could almost cut it with a knife. I lay there stunned. It lasted a long time. It was as if I were breathing in his love, smelling it, and drinking it in every pore of my body. I would never be the same. I knew from that moment on that what they leave behind is a field of love. And in so many ways a deeper, more intense kind of love that being in the body. This is impossible to convey in words. While in spirit we become unconditional love.

If we love ourselves and our loved ones, we know they go on without attachment or outcome, even in death. For in reality there is no death. We all are energy. We are made of light, but when the matter stops, when we stop breathing, we do not stop. It is a fact that energy cannot be destroyed. So if we are energy that means that the true self cannot be gone. It is recycled It goes to somewhere else. It turns into another form like water heated turns into steam.

Why do we suffer over our losses? It is because we "think" of them as losses. Do we cry over each day that leaves us in the twilight? No, instead we love watching the sun go down because of the beauty of the sun going past the horizon and the colors it leave in the sky. Do we grieve the end of a meal and all the food is finished and is in our bodies to give us nourishment? We are not attached to these things. We have learned that these are all a part of our everyday life. When the sun goes it come back the next day and the food we eat give us the strength to live and that there will be more to eat the next day. So why is it that we do not learn that when we die it is not the end but the beginning of a new life? It is that our loved ones are not gone, just like the food in our bodies has gone to a different place in a new form. And in most cases, they are more accessible to us on a daily basis. There are no miles to drive or phone calls to make.

So we grieve and suffer their loss. Suffering comes from thought. We are taught to suffer and to believe that to lose someone or something is a terrible thing. But is it so horrible? We may lose a job but there may be a better opportunity around the corner or a whole new career. People we care about may turn their backs on us and go from us, but there are over seven billion people on this planet so there are new wonderful people to meet. The list is endless as is the whole concept. Our life is all about change. And life is a flow of constant changes and constant opportunities. And there is endless hope.

Letting go can feel like a loss. That's because it is. But every loss paves the way for a gain, if we're willing to receive it. Every time we let something go, we open ourselves up to something better.
(Lori Deschene)

Let us learn to be mindful and aware. We must learn to be more still and in the moment. Whatever comes our way we deal with it as it comes. So when we "think", we have an endless chatter in our heads. We analyze, judge, criticize, plan, and make decisions. Thinking is remembering, reflecting, solving problems, and more.

What lies behind us and what lies before us are tiny matters compared to what lies within us.
(Oliver Wendell Holmes)

So this leads me back to the matter of our bodies and our DNA. Within us is great strength, great knowledge, all knowledge; we have great inspiration, great emotion, great power. We have the power to change and know the principles of the Universe. There is so much more to us than we know in this world. By studying and listening to the wise and holy people of the earth, we can connect with places we never dreamed we could go while on this earth.

Gregg Braden, author and scientist, says *"All matter originates and exists by virtue of a Force. We must assume behind this force is a conscious, intelligent Matrix"* (quoting Max Planck).

Gregg Braden has studied and traveled the world for answers to these places inside us and outside us. On the web site DNA Discoveries—Gregg Braden, 2004 12 15, he tells us about the great experiments he and his colleagues did with emotion and DNA.

Gregg Braden says we are forced to accept the possibility that some NEW field of energy, a web of energy, is there and the DNA is communicating with the photons through this energy. These emotional changes went beyond the effects of electromagnetics. Individuals trained in deep love were able to change the shape of their DNA. Gregg Braden says this illustrates a new recognized form of energy that connects all of creation. This energy appears to be a TIGHTLY WOVEN WEB that connects all of creation. This energy appears to be a TIGHTLY WOVEN WEB that connects all matter. Essentially we're able to influence this web of creation through our VIBRATION.

It is my belief and many others' today that our DNA is that large transmitter with this field Braden is talking about. And if that is the case we see that love, faith, and HOPE are a part of this field, and it can even change the matter of our bodies from within.

Let us not despair about anything in this world. Let us stand firm in belief that all is taken care of and that we all have the capacity to live on no matter what befalls us because it is written inside of our heart, literally. Hope is not a pie in the sky concept; it is about what life is based.

If you think you are suffering because you are dying, that is a mistake. Nobody dies. There is no such thing as death. There is only eternal life and you are THAT.
(Sri Ramana Maharishi)

When we think we are our bodies, we will always suffer. But when we come to the realization that we are a soul, a spirit, we no longer need to suffer. The spirit lives in the moment and is spontaneous and filled with joy in the present. The present is all that matters. When something or some condition comes into your life, you respond in the moment and let it go, moving into what comes in the next moment. You are run by the engine of your true self—spirit—and life reveals itself to you, not you organizing and controlling your life. The mind no longer has dominance in your life. The mind is there to keep the body running and make decisions for us without thought. When we are run by spirit, through the heart, we are truly beings of eternal life right here on earth.

I had returned to my home town for the memorial of a dear old friend. I came back to Sedona and life. One morning I was making my bed when she came up in my mind. Immediately, my thoughts went to my never seeing her again. Then the emotion of sorrow welled up in me. However, I stopped and thought to myself. "You know better than this. You are looking and searching in the wrong place. Yes, she is physically gone and I will not see her on earth but she is still alive. I must search for her in that place which I know is always available."

When we go into the thought of never seeing them again we are attached to the physical. Sorrow comes and we are caught in a spiral of despair. We finally get out of it and move on until it arrives again. It becomes a cycle that appears over and over. Suffering becomes a choice.

Sometimes after the loss of a significant other we think of going with them, we think of suicide. We think of this for many reasons. The fact that we cannot imagine life without them, that the pain of losing them is so great, we cannot stand it. We know they are in another realm but we want to be with them. What we really want is to be in a place of love and happiness again. The physical seems to be too painful. But if we can open our hearts and minds this world is here for us even as we are alive.

Think on this: this world is not the original world. This is the dream and illusion. The primary world is the spirit world. This is the place of form and creativity. Now you must change your mind from one of attachment to one of the non-physical, the place of "no matter", The Place Called Hope, the spiritual world. It is a place. So you now change to searching for them in the spirit world. Getting to this point is difficult but necessary for acceptance of their passing from this world to next.

How do you do this? Next time you miss your loved one think of the love you had. Remember love, not the physical body. Feel the love they had for you and you for them. Hold on to the love and stay in that. That is the spiritual realm. We are all made of Love and light. This is now where they reside. Hold on to remembering the love and soon you will not be remembering but actually feeling them in the present and their love for you now. You have now found the Place Called Hope.

All the things that truly matter—beauty, love, creativity, joy, inner peace— arise from beyond the mind.
(Eckhart Tolle)

The illusion is that we are only physical.

(Vanna Bonta)

Our experience tells us that our reality is made up of physical material things, and that our world is an independently existing objective one. Again, what quantum mechanics reveals is that there is no true "physicality" in the universe, that atoms are made of focused vortices of energy-miniature tornadoes that are constantly popping into and out of existence. The revelation that the universe is not an assembly of physical parts, suggested by Newtonian physics, and instead comes from a holistic entanglement of immaterial energy waves stems the works of Albert Einstein, Max Planck, and Werner Heisenberg, among others.

(Arjun Walia)

Part VI

The Matter of Our Physical Body

The Matter of Our Body

**The human body is vapor materialized by
sunshine mixed with the life of the stars.**

(Paracelsus)

The atom, being for all practical purposes the stable unit of the physical plane, is a constantly changing vortex of reactions.

(Kabbalah)

Mass that occupies space is matter. Something that has mass and exists as a solid, liquid, gas, or plasma is a thing in matter. And Lawrence Turner of STACKS Online Library states it as; "That of which the sensible universe and all existent bodies are composed; anything which has extension, occupies space, or is perceptible by the senses; body; substance."

In ancient times the four elements earth, water, air and fire were looked at as the ingredients for alchemy. Alchemy brings to mind magic and the mysterious. However, this was "science" before mankind knew of such a complex concept. The entire material world was made of these four elements, including our bodies. The modern day explanations of these elements concerning mass are solids, liquids, gases and heat in science.

The Chinese say there is a Fifth element. In the movie of the same name, the fifth element manifests on earth in a time of great need to the planet. To save the world the four elements must do their thing but the fifth element is in the center of the square made by the four; a beacon of light is emitted from the very matter of the body of a woman who is supposed to hold the fifth element in her body. Because of these five together, all evil is stopped. Of course this just a movie but it is what the ancient Chinese taught, that the fifth element is the light that burns in us all and the very "life force". Whereas the four elements make up the world of matter the fifth element GIVES life to the matter. We live in a shell of matter that is our physical body. This is composed of all atoms and molecules that make up the cells. We have the five senses that let us move through the world and operate. The matter of our body is our vehicle to let us do what our mind creates and what our heart desires.

As suggested above, plasma is one of elements of mass, it is so common in the universe. We have plasma in our bodies! The word plasma is associated with our blood. Our blood is a carrier of oxygen to our organs. The cells need the oxygen to live. The smallest unnoticed part of our lives, air and breathing, are what holds up the basis of our being, even our DNA. The surface of blood cells have an electrochemical property; it carries an electrical charge and is sensitive to electromagnetic fields. If one would place a magnet under a slide with our blood on the slide and then look through a microscope you would see all of the cells lined up relative to the magnetic field. So when we breathe we oxygenate our blood, and this combined with the electrical charge of the magnetic fields, we create the charge that keeps us alive. It is in effect the principle of fire, the fire of Life.

Life, according to Eastern thought, manifests through fire. They believe that it is this concept that is the beginning of all "matter". In our culture science will tell us life comes from "matter". The chicken before the egg or the egg before the chicken, I am not sure, but I do know that when we breathe we create life with each and every breath. This is invisible to the naked eye but very much necessary to our existence.

The photosynthesis of light by plastids in plants is not only important for plants but for all living matter. In the animal world the cell's energy is produced in mitochondria. The Encyclopedia Britannica defines mitochondria as: "*Often called the powerhouses of the cell, the sausage-shaped mitochondria produce the energy needed by the cell to junction. Food molecules that pass into the cytoplasm are taken into the mitochondria and oxidized, or burned for energy. Like plastids, mitochondria have an inner and an outer membrane. Also like plastids, they depend upon the cell's DNA or certain proteins.*" These mitochondria are like transistors, providing energy or power to the entire cell. There is a biochemical response to the cells with DNA. Our DNA is like a biochemical emissary within our being. This is the place where we correspond with the entirety of the earth and the universe. In *Energy Matter and Form: Toward a Science of Consciousness*, Christopher Hills tells us, "*The degree to which the mitochondria vibrate in rhythm or harmonic resonance with the surrounding environmental field determines the ability of each cell to crystallize or trap the etheric life energy to which our body owes its physical existence, and by which we gain increased sensitivity to and awareness of life itself.*"

I am a soul with a body rather than a body with a soul.

(Unknown)

While there is life, there is hope.

(Cicero)

So where is Hope in all of this and why the matter of Hope? How can a spiritual concept like Hope live in matter? And what does it have to do with loss, change, and/or the death of loved one? We see there is a fine line between our emotions, mind and body. In fact it is not linear at all, but circular in nature. One affects the other and can not do without the other.

The very nature of Hope and spiritual virtues do dwell in the matter of our body. Our mind can transform grief and depression into the beacon of Hope through a disciplined effort, changed perception, and commitment.

The physical world, including our bodies, is a response of the observer.

We create our bodies as we create the experience of our world.

(Deepak Chopra)

Breathing

**Breathe deeply and gently through every cell of the body,
laugh happily, and release the head of all worries and anxieties;
and finally breathe in the blessing of
love and, hope that Is flowing in the air,
and you will understand the meaning of the human breath.**

(Pundit Acharya)

Breath represents the movement of spirit in matter.

(Andrew Weil, M.D.)

There are events in life that leave us breathless. Being surprised or seeing something of beauty or falling in love are some of the positive events. However, when it comes to losing someone or something that has been a part of us, this leaves us not only breathless but feeling as if each breath is an effort.

It is the most basic of all physical actions. Breathing is life and there is no life without it. It can relax us, clear our head and provide strength when we focus on it. Taking deep breathes during a time of stress is sometimes all we can do.

No longer do we live in the West with exclusive western concepts of healing and medicine. Many Western doctors are adding to their practices such things as alternative healing, herbs, and yoga. Dr. Andrew Weil of the Center for Integrative Medicine, in Tucson Arizona, really believes in giving the healing process over to the patient. He incorporates a healthy diet, exercise, spiritual and mental exercises and yoga.

Yoga has been used for centuries. Before we had medications people of the world used methods like breath work to help calm and energize themselves.

In *Hindu-Yogi Science of Breath* when Ramacharaka says one may, by controlled breathing *"practically do away with fear and worry and the baser emotions,"* he refers to the growing ability of a devoted practitioner to diminish the power which both momentary and permanent fears have over us. One seeks to develop habits of resistance to the disturbing effects of excitement, ambition, antagonism and frustration.

In Yoga, theory and practice, as well as left brain and right brain, go hand in hand so to speak. Study (svâdhyâya) is in fact an important aspect of many branches and schools of Yoga. This is another way in which Yoga's balanced approach shows itself.
(George Feuerstein)

So you can understand why the use of Yoga or breathing exercises for our work with the Matter of Hope is useful. The importance of the balance of the left and right brains gives us balance. Yoga and breath work is one of the many tools we can use to aid in that balance.

As you breathe, acknowledge your thoughts, feelings and emotions as you inhale and then release them as you exhale. Stay aware of your breathing and focus only on it.

Body positions for breathing exercise:
Place your feet on the floor. Sit up straight. Rest your arms on your thighs or by your side, palms up, thumb and index finger touching. The palms up position roll your shoulder joints open. The thumb and index finger touching creates a balance between mind and body.

1. Breathing with head bowed:
Keeping your eyes closed; bring your chin to your chest. Take a long breath and exhale; do this 3 times. Then slowly bring your neck to its upright position by uncurling it one vertebra at a time.

2. Nostril breathing:
This time use your left hand to push your left nostril shut. Now take a deep breath and hold it. Then release the nostril as you exhale through your mouth. Now use your right hand to shut your right nostril and do the same process of breathing. Do each nostril 3 times.

3. General Position:
Place your feet on the floor. Sit up straight. Rest your arms on your thighs or by your side, palms up, thumbs and index finger touching. With the palms up position, roll your shoulder joints open. The thumb and index finger touching creates a balance between mind and body.

Stay aware of your physical and emotional needs throughout the exercises. Tuning in to the body is the only way to tune up the body.

Recall a time that would have caused you to forget that hope is at the bottom of the earthen vessel. What happened in you life, or which one of the negative sufferings that were set loose by Pandora, blocked your view of Hope.

Name it and write it down.

How does your body feel when you recall all of this?

Begin to release all the tension in your body, inhaling deeply, filling your stomach and lungs. Slowly push the breath out of your upper lungs, mid-lungs, lower lungs and belly. Do this 3 times.

Relaxation

Now we will do a relaxation exercise. As a hypnotherapist this is the first thing I do in a session. Relaxation is the beginning of all healing.

(You may want to read this first and then recall what you read. Or you may have someone read this to you or make your own recording of this exercise.)

Take a deep breath and hold it; release it slowly. Close your eyes and listen to the beat of your heart. Sit in silence for a few seconds and listen. Now see a golden light over your head. Let this light come down over your head, down the front of your forehead, around the entire front of your face, relaxing all the muscles in your face, release tension around your mouth and your chin, now your jaw.

Feel the warmth down the back of your scalp and down to the back of your neck, feel the warm light spread in both directions on your shoulder blades and down your spine, slowly and gently, one vertebra at a time, slowly, now down the spine, feeling more and more relaxed, let the tension go.

Now go back to the front to body, to the shoulders and let them release, let the muscles go, feeling more and more relaxed, feel the warmth spread down your torso to your stomach and abdomen. Feel all the tension, feel the muscles in your stomach, go down to your hips and feel the warmth go all the way around to the back of your buttocks and let all the muscles go. Feeling more and more relaxed.

Now let the muscles in your legs go, spread the warmth, go down your thighs all around to the back of your thighs and then your knees, down to your calves and release all the muscles, feel relaxed down around your ankles and all around the foot, the bottom of the foot and to your toes, now feeling totally relaxed, you are totally relaxed and feel good, feeling happy and peaceful.

Now see a balloon and in that balloon are all the worries and suffering that you recall that have kept you from having hope. See them locked inside the balloon away from you, not inside of your mind and heart any longer. See yourself holding the string attached to the balloon, hold the balloon up and let the string go, see the balloon float away from you. Watch it slowly drift off into the sky, see it slowly and gently go farther and father up into the sky, watch as it blows away so far that you can no longer see it. It is gone. No more stress, Feeling happy and relaxed, knowing there is hope and that you can feel good.

Sit a second and see all the wonderful things you would like to do or to accomplish, listen to your heart beating, listen to your breath. Now feeling relaxed, all tension gone, mind clear and emotions calm, now slowly and gently come back to opening your eyes. Now slowly open your eyes and know you are relaxed and calm.

Take time to do this as often as you can, releasing all the stress.

Take the time daily to check your breathing. If you can not do the relaxation you can do the breathing. Breath is life, and begin to focus and be thankful!

Physical Effects of Loss

Your body is precious. It is our vehicle for awakening. Treat it with care.

(Buddha)

Our body goes through a tremendous shock when we lose a loved one or have a serious trauma. It is plain old stress and of the most challenging kind. We will find that our memory goes, that blood pressure will go up or down, and it is difficult to breathe. Here are some other physical symptoms you may experience: physical exhaustion, uncontrollable crying, disruption of sleep, chest pain, headaches, recurrent infections, loss of appetite, stomach upsets, aches and pains, hair loss, disruption of the menstrual cycle, irritability, worsening of any chronic condition such as eczema or asthma.

With loss the very matter of our physical body can change. I remember shortly after my brother's death I started to have stomach pains. It was months after his passing, so I never imagined it was from my grief. My doctor called it a nervous stomach and gave me pills. It disappeared as I began to deal with the grief on a deeper level. With the loss of my daughter it was hard to tell what developed from the complicated birth process and from the grief. Even today over 20 years later I have health problems. When the loss is extreme and we are not ready it can create life long health problems for you. Loss is a part of life. Each and everyday we are losing to the clock. How we deal with it on a mental and physical level will tell the quality of our life. The emotions, mind and body are intertwined and it is hard to separate them when dealing with despair and loss.

Stress of loss leaves our body in an unbalanced state. It leaves the body weakened from the mind telling the body something terrible has happened. The hope and miracle of our matter is that built into our DNA is the answer to all healing. It goes as deep as that. Doctors may know how to fight infections and heal broken bones, but a real healer understands that our bodies are made to do it on their own. In his book, *Spontaneous Healing*, Dr. Andrew Weil speaks about the DNA and its ability to heal: "*Healing is spontaneous. It is a natural tendency arising from the internal nature of DNA. The occurrence of a lesion automatically activates the process of its repair. In larger pattern of biological organization in human beings these same characteristics obtain. As above, so below; as below, so above.*"

Dr. Weil goes on at the end of this chapter on healing using grief as a model to talk about the mind and healing. He agrees that any loss whether it is a job, a pet or a loved one really is a reminder of our own demise. He tells us that the shock and denial is a kind of sedative to our bodies and minds. After working through all the emotions of loss, we finally come to acceptance. And finally he has this to say, "*We might argue about where emotional healing fits into the subject . Is it higher or lower than healing at the level of body systems? Is mind the highest expression of genetic information encoded in DNA or manifestation of a field of consciousness underlying matter including DNA? As above, so below; as below, so above.*"

I believe our DNA is not only the 'road map' to our entire body structure for healing and building but it has a spiritual formula that is what the good doctor speaks about. Could it be that our DNA is the receptor to the universe? And that all faith, hope and love is written into our matter?

See! I will not forget you. I have carved you on the palm of my hand.

(Isaiah 49:15)

Our DNA: The Key

If a signature from our Creator has, in fact, survived the elements of time and nature, then it makes perfect sense that the sign would remain within our bodies.

(Gregg Braden)

My husband and I created the matter of Hope, our daughter. In 1993 I gave birth to a baby girl, and in minutes, she passed on. She was born with a genetic defect of her DNA; Trisomy 13. The statistics on the chances of having a child with this defect are 1 out of 21,000. Why us? And how could this happen? She was not perfect; or was she? "*Trisomy 13 Syndrome is a rare chromosomal disorder in which all or a portion of chromosome 13 appears three times (trisomy) rather than twice in cells of the body. In some affected individuals, only a percentage of cells may contain the extra 13th chromosome (mosaicism), whereas other cells contain the normal chromosomal pair.*" (National Organization for Rare Disorders)

So what is DNA? "*Short for deoxyribonucleic acid. The nucleic acid that is the genetic material determining the makeup of all living cells and many viruses.*" (Free Dictionary)

From the National Health Museum, Classic Collect; *The Structure of the DNA Molecule*, we learn of the first discovery of the structure of our DNA: "*In 1951, the then 23-year old biologist James Watson traveled from the United States to work with Francis Crick, an English physicist at the University of Cambridge. Crick was already using the process of X-ray crystallography to study the structure of protein molecules. Together, Watson and Crick used X-ray crystallography data, produced by Rosalind Franklin and Maurice Wilkins at King's College in London, to decipher DNA's structure.*"

What they learned was it was made up of four molecules; adenine (a purine), cytosine (a pyrimidine), guanine (a purine), thymine (a pyrimidine). Watson and Crick worked with a wire structure as a model, to place these molecules on this wire to see what the structure became. Here is what they wrote: "*This (DNA) structure has two helical chains each, coiled round the same axis. Both chains follow right-handed helices; the two chains run in opposite directions; The bases are on the inside of the helix and the phosphates on the outside.*"

DNA is what makes us who we are. The very fact that our daughter had a DNA defect led me down Alice's Rabbit Hole. And we wanted answers. Was it my family, his family or how could there be a defect on the DNA? I had to learn about it all. So I went looking in the world and within myself.

How much does science really know about our bodies? Medical doctors will tell us they have made miraculous strides in knowledge. But ask a Chinese Medicine doctor or acupuncturist the same question and you will get a different answer. After I had my daughter the effects on my body were long lasting. Doctors told me my blood pressure from the preclampsia would go down but it never did. Over twenty years later I have health problems from carrying Hope and giving her life. As a result, I wanted to try something outside of Western medicine. I decided I would see an acupuncturist and a Chinese Medicine doctor. Medical science and Chinese medicine see things in a very different way. I doctor with both and it has been difficult balancing it all.

> *Traditional Chinese medicine is a broad range of medicine practices sharing common concepts which have been developed in China and are based on a tradition of more than 2,000 years, including various forms of herbal medicine, acupuncture, massage (Tua na), exercise (qigong) and dietary therapy.*
>
> (Wikipedia)

When I visit my acupuncturist and talk in "disease" terms he will usually correct me by talking about what the symptoms are or where the pain is. Chinese medicine does not focus on disease. The belief system is that the body can cure itself if aided to be put back in balance.

> *Western medicine is based on the Cartesian philosophy that the body represents one functioning system and the mind another. It accepts that each system may affect the other, but essentially it sees disease as either physical or mental. The Chinese assume that the body is whole, and each part of it is intimately connected. Each organ has a mental as well as a physical function.*
>
> (George T. Lewith MA, MRCGP, MRCP)

Chinese medicine began in the second century B.C. It is not easily accepted by Western medicine but has begun to get respect. Both have qualities that work and Western medicine could learn a lot from this ancient method of healing. On the web site "China Highlights" they tell us about the first doctor in China to bring all the ancient knowledge together. The Bencao Gengmu is the most important traditional work on herbs and drugs. It was written in the middle of the Ming Dynasty era (1368-1644) by Li Shizhen (1518-1593). He was a doctor and former official of the Imperial Medical Bureau of the Ming Empire. He studied herbs, minerals and animal parts. He also studied information on geology, physics and other topics and pulled it together to make long lists of healing research for others to use. It was considered the greatest contribution of the Ming era.

Over time some of what has known about our bodies has been lost or disregarded. Varying cultures over time have kept knowledge away from each other. Chinese medicine is ancient and yet little was known to the western world for centuries. And now, when it is known, it is slowly being acknowledged. The point is science is still learning about our bodies and how it works. Each year more and more is known. And yet we know nothing about how our bodies and spirits work together.

Ask a scientist to tell you about your spirit. More than likely they will tell you that having a spirit has never been proven. Psychology is the field of study where they would study the spirit. On line The Scientific Proof Of The Existence Of The Soul Wednesday, February 27, 2013 states: *"Psychology is defined as 'the study of the soul', yet doctors have trouble defining the Soul. Webster's defines soul as 'the immortal essence, animating principle, or an activating cause of an individual life.' But medical science is divided between the soul/mind and the brain/consciousness as the essence of the human psyche. In 1901 Dr. Duncan MacDougall determined that the soul weighed 21 grams by weighing dying patient's right before and right after death."* There is very little known on this subject. How does this all fit together, body, mind, and spirit?

Just months after losing my daughter, my husband and I met a woman who gave us a VHS tape. It was an underground tape of a video conversation with scientists who were studying the structure of our DNA and its relationship to anthropology and language. It seems this scientist, in the video, had been doing studies in patterns in languages. As with most of the great discoveries in science, he came up with his idea from boredom, or what I like to say, when he relaxed, the information presented itself. He stopped working and started reading from Genesis. Why not study the first few versus of Genesis? He then realized that what he was looking at in the Bible was what he needed to study. He spoke of mathematics as the basis of the Hebrew alphabet; each letter has a numerical value. What about the number values in the first few versus of the Bible? What must that be?

What he found led him to a brand new discovery. He got a copy of the Torah, as original as he could find. He took each Hebrew letter and put the numerical values to each. As he did this, a definite pattern and equation appeared. Then he went a step further. He decided to do an equation that gave a third-dimensional form to the pattern. Lo and behold the pattern was the double helix, the shape of the DNA strand. And now today, others are stepping forward to say they too have found the same thing. The writers of the Old Testament Bible did write in code the language of mathematics. It was the code of third-dimensional shape of the molecules of our very being. It was mind blowing to me, and I am sure it was the catalyst to that which I have perceived today.

This video and the knowledge stayed with me. Then years later, my story in the Tree of Life, where I wrote about the letter Beth (Bet). Beth is the first letter of the first word in the Bible; *be-Rashith means "in the beginning", Remember, it is used to represent creation. A house is a container for the household; consequently, Binah, the Great Mother, is considered to hold her creation of all of the lower worlds in her womb. It also is meaning the "mouth" of man. Whatever goes into the body to nourish it, it then sends "the words of life" out through the mouth. The vocal cords and mouth are used and Beth lies there with the mystery of the Word Transcendent. It is also the number 2.* I was born on January 2nd. Was I being told to write and to speak of this? But I digress.

Today, it is common knowledge that this spiral structure is DNA strands. It is upon this structure our individual pattern is laid down. At the time of this writing, science only knows 10% of what that double helix really does. 90% of it has yet to be determined as to its function. Our basic DNA never changes.

My theory is that this DNA structure is encoded with the Divine Grace and Energy that makes mankind's DNA perfect. I also think the DNA traits of man is golden light as was stated in all the legends and myths of mankind's cultures about the Garden. The Garden is within us; in our DNA, our Tree of Life and Knowledge. It is encoded with all goodness, and I believe all the traits of a Creator—compassion, kindness, love, and hope. It is our experiences that turn us away from this inborn information and spiritual connection to our Creator. The good news is that it is always here, within us, to assess when we choose to reach for it.

DNA is like a computer. I believe all knowledge and everything we want to know lies within. The answers to all of the universe and our Creator are locked inside the cells of our matter. The Creator made it our operating system. But we do not know how it works. I believe when we are born, our DNA is purely flooded in Grace, the Divine Energy. We are programmed within this double helix with all the virtues known to man; kindnesses, compassion, loyalty, trust, and so on. We have heard it said in the text of all religions, and by the holy people of the Earth, "Look within for the answers." Of course, we have taken this statement to mean to go inside in prayer and contemplation, to think on the larger questions for ourselves. I believe they knew that it quite literally meant, inside of us, not only our mind and spirit, but that all knowledge lives in the matter of our body.

Using the metaphor of the computer: because we do not know how to use the operating system we just guess at how it works. Also because we are not aware of how to use it once we are in the world, influenced by experiences and patterns we become negative, we lose our connection to this place in ourselves within that DNA. It is from our heritage and individual choices we separate from that goodness and the knowledge we have been given at birth.

Children are innocent and are still in direct connection with this aspect of themselves. Jesus said, "Come to me as little children." What did he mean? I think he meant to go to that place in ourselves that knows the truth, the very matter of our pure being where all knowledge and goodness abides. Innocence is the key. Worldly knowledge is the separator. The DNA is the antenna. the heart feels, and mind is not to be used to think but to translate what the heart feels and information from the nature of our psychical bodies give us. Everything flows with ease and there is nothing that needs to be studied because it is all within each of us. Does a plant think? Do cats and cows not know who they are and where they are to live and what to do? Why are we any different?

Alberto Villoldo tells us "*Shamans live in a world where the Creator is not separate from the Creation, Heaven is not separate from Earth, and Spirit and matter infuse each other.*" There is no division between the body and the spirit, nor between the visible world of form and the invisible world of energy. Everything is energy and vibration, and I believe that these strands that make our being have frequencies that can transform not only our mind but our spirit. Our planet is based on electromagnetic energy. Our bodies are no different. Our bodies resonate at a level of 0.1 Hz to 30 Hz in the brain. These are the electromagnetic brain waves. The Earth has an electromagnetic resonance as well. It measures at 7.5 Hz to 30 Hz. The brain vibrates at different levels at different activities. Sleeping is .5 Hz to 35 Hz, and head pain is 13 Hz to 30 Hz, whereas intense mental concentration is 14 Hz to 30 Hz. We are, in a sense, an electromagnetic generator.

Susan Alexjander and Dr. David Dreamer have studied and experimented with the frequency of DNA. Some of their studies have come up with DNA resonance at a wavelength of 321/702 Nanometers. They tested the chemicals that make up our DNA, and the bases and their frequencies they found were: Adenine: 545.6 Hz, Guanine: 550 Hz, Thymine: 543.4 Hz, and Cytosine: 537.8 Hz.

Time Shift: The Experience of Dimensional Change by Janet I. Sussman states: "*The DNA molecule is probably the most sensitive and complex molecule in the Universe. It is capable of restructuring when it is aligned with external frequencies, which have the power to reprogram it. With practice, as our perception becomes more refined, we become capable of synchronizing with the Earth's Schumann frequency, which is reported to be increasing from 7.8 up to 13 Hertz. Our intelligence and wisdom of thought, action, feeling, and compassion become speeded up as we assume our rightful role as holograms of infinite consciousness. We become able to transmit and receive the inspirational wave frequencies (Morphic Fields) of archives of the higher dimension (Akasha) thus nourishing and being nourished by them. The pathways to the higher intelligence of the Causal Plane can open, and the mind/spirit becomes capable of locating itself.*"

The double tetrahedron creates a spiral. In ancient history, this figure, or symbol, has presented itself over and over again. Spirals are found in all of the holy places on the Earth. It is said that these are portals to the other side of the veil of existence, or the other dimensions. There are spirals drawn and etched into stone and temples all over the world. And so it is for us, within every spec of our bodies, a portal to the other dimensions.

The world's cultures and religions have used symbols to represent the things of earthly matter, as well as the spiritual realm. Shamans used symbols to transcend the ego and travel to other worlds, in altered states. During this altered state, the shaman could heal. There are dances to this day that tribes perform in swirls and spiral shapes to create a state of transcendence. How did they know about the spiral being a part of our very being? We have only learned this fact, but humans before the time of technology had knowledge because they went within or to nature for the answers. Have we lost the ability to do this? Or do we believe in the outer world to give us what we need instead of believing in ourselves?

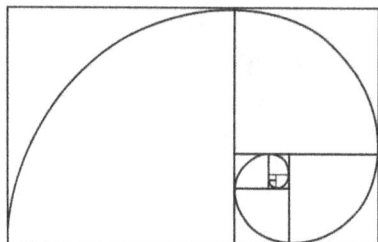

Have you seen this figure before? Yes, it is a spiral. This is called the Golden Mean Spiral. There are many examples of the Golden Section or Divine Proportion in Nature. Phi is frequently expressed in many of Nature's creations, and by varying the angle between adjacent radii, a number of natural spirals and leaf shapes can be created. The Fibonacci numbers form the best whole number approximations to the Golden number.

By definition, the first two numbers in the Fibonacci sequence are 1 and 1, or 0 and 1, depending on the chosen starting point of the sequence, and each subsequent number is the sum of the previous two.

(Wikipedia)

Plants illustrate the Fibonacci series in the numbers and arrangements of petals, leaves, sections and seeds. Plants that are formed in spirals, such as pinecones, pineapples and sunflowers, illustrate Fibonacci numbers. Many plants produce new branches in quantities that are based on Fibonacci numbers.

Posted by Brett Dusek on March 8, 2009: *"Golden ratio is an irrational mathematical constant that represents the ratio of one quantity to another quantity. Golden ratio is given the value of 1.6180339887, and continues on infinitely. You can find this value in nature, universal bodies (such as galaxies), artwork, architecture, literature and many other area of interest. To some it is merely an insignificant coincidence, to others it is a number of vast importance, interconnecting life, matter and the universe."*

The first work on the golden mean is often attributed to Theano, wife of Pythagorus. The poet John Keats, in his "Ode on a Grecian Urn", put it this way: *"Beauty is truth, truth is beauty that is all Ye know on earth, and all Ye need to know."*

To the Greek mentality, it was an attribute of beauty. Both ancients and moderns realized that "there is a close association in mathematics between beauty and truth." The Greeks believed there to be three 'ingredients' to beauty: symmetry, proportion, and harmony. This triad of principles infused their life. They were very much attuned to beauty as an object of love and something that was to be imitated and reproduced in their lives, architecture, and politics.

We see spirals in nature: tornados and dirt devils in the desert, ferns when they first come up are tightly compressed spirals, water goes down the drain in a spiral. As I was researching the material for this section, I came across Sedona, Arizona, which is where I sit writing to you from my home. I forgot to include the place right under my nose! The Earth has spiraling vortices of energy, electromagnetic energy, and in Sedona, there are several intense vortices. It is said to be a holy place to the Native Americans and a high energy spiritual place.

Today, we know that symbols can access places in our psyche that we cannot reach using normal means. They have been used to release blocks for traumas and release memory of suppressed emotions. Jung thought of symbols as being the way we can access the unconscious and that inward journey of what I speak. When we are ready to heal, we need to find those places we have hidden to tend to them as we would wounds.

Labyrinths and spiral mazes are ancient. In olden times, these huge monuments were thought to help you clear and balance your mind. Jeff Saward, the editor of Caerdroia tells us, "*In all the labyrinths seems to symbolize the path to be followed in daily and seasonal cycles, in life and in death, and in rebirth. Beyond all these may exist a cosmology, an ancient understanding of the cycles of time, all safely concealed within the labyrinth, locked up in numbers and movements.*" Again, these are symbols you could walk upon and create a new point of view or enter into a state of bliss. They could possibly move us to the higher vibration of our DNA.

There are myths and symbols that carry the spiral throughout history. The Caduceus dates back as far as Sumerian times and I believe before that time. And this one has stuck with us to this very day. It is the symbol of healing, such as Registered Nurses in the United States and other health agencies:

Legend tells us this was taken from Greek mythology. The symbolic representation of two intertwined snakes appeared early in Babylonia and is related to other serpent symbols of fertility, wisdom, and healing, and of sun gods. This staff of Hermes was carried by Greek heralds and ambassadors and became a Roman mark for truce, neutrality, and noncombatant status.

This symbol means a fusion of opposites involved in the healing process. However, it is directly the same structure in the Kabbalah with its central staff and the two pillars and pathways that cross over the central area several times. We must all realize that cultures have borrowed images, symbols, and rituals throughout time. Each culture will use the symbol to suit their needs and perceptions. It will not necessarily have the same meaning as when it was originally created.

There are also synchronicities. In all cultures, similar stories and symbols emerge at the same time without the exchange of knowledge. In the Eastern religions, the staff can mean the spine and the snakes carrying the Kundalini energy, or life force up the spine. This symbol can be seen on Hindu temples representing this serpent energy of yoga. The Kundalini is the lower human aspects, the earthly part of us as it moves up the spine. Our spine directs the flow of energy in our bodies.

Eastern medicine has given us the seven chakras and 21 minor chakras that are the energy receptors in our bodies. These centers spin in a clockwise, circular fashion. And as energy works inwardly, it becomes a spiral effect. The chakras deal with the lower emotions in the lower areas of the body, and in the heart and higher up in the body are the higher emotions that DNA transmutes into the spiritual aspects of us. This matches the Tree of Life of the Kabbalah.

Among archetypal images, the Sacred Tree is one of the most widely known symbols on earth. There are few cultures in which the Sacred Tree does not figure: as a image of the cosmos, as a dwelling place of Gods or spirits, as a medium of prophecy and knowledge, and as an agent of metamorphoses when the tree is transformed into human or divine form or when it bears a divine or human imagine as its fruit or flowers.

(Christopher McDowell)

The place where Hope sits on the Tree of Life (Kabbalah) is a field between our thoughts and emotions on the lower level. But it sits right next to the place that holds the essence of who we are, and that transmits the information to move on up the road to the spiritual parts of us. We cannot enter that field if we continue to live in the lower emotions of sorrow, anger, depression, and more. It is hard for us to get to love, mercy, and faith; we must go through the Way of Hope. Waking our will to live and expressing those lower emotions and knowing that hope holds endless possibilities to change us, transmutes us physically. This is the stuff of physics, light, and energy. The DNA must be built with light and energy; these too are matter.

Every fiber in our being is encoded with DNA. Every strand of hair, flecks of skin, every part of us has our unique blueprint. However, the framework, or structure, of DNA is the same in all of mankind. It is the pattern on the structure that makes us unique. When a child is conceived, the cells begin to divide and grow. The chromosomes from the parents give the sex of the child and give the blueprint, or pattern, of the DNA for that child. There is selection made from the 20,000 to 25,000 genes in human DNA that make each person unique.

Mutation happens in DNA spontaneously, but also in response to environmental changes that occur over time, such as climate change. This change not only happens to the land, it can also change the DNA of all the living beings who live there. Perhaps the DNA of the individuals who live in an area affected by change will evolve.

As I have said, I believe on each strand in our cells, is a Divine transmitter, so to speak. It is all laid out for us. The stuff of the Creator makes us Creators. We have it in our DNA. Emotions are given as buffers for the mental aspects and to deal with trauma from this physical plane. They are warning systems and give us ways to express the Divine in matter. Emotions are to be discovered and felt. They are momentary and not to be held onto for any length of time. In a new magazine publication called "What is Enlightenment", James Gardner, a physicist, talks about a revolutionary hypothesis that dovetails with my theory. He says the theory is that nature and the cosmos has a pattern, which is not just random, but a definite plan. Gardner quotes another scientist, Paul Davies, who says the following:

If life follows from primordial soup with causal dependability, the laws of nature encode a hidden subtext, a cosmic imperative, which tells them "Make life," and through life its byproducts, mind, knowledge, understanding ... it means that the laws of the universe have engineered their own comprehension. This is a breathtaking vision of nature!

Gardner goes on and makes his own comments about what Davies had to say, "*This vision says that intelligence is built into the physical laws of nature. It is saying that the emergence of life and intelligence is preprogrammed."* For me, it means what I believe to be true about our DNA, which has ALL information that is also connected to the patterns in nature. Also, our DNA is only a part of the larger DNA of the earth. So it means that there is a consciousness in nature and in the DNA itself. Remember, physics now states that there must be an "observer" for anything to come into matter. These theories imply that human DNA and nature have a consciousness that is the "observer", which then manifests just because it had observed its own beginnings. It truly means that in matter everything is connected. As the Bible states, God is everywhere and in everything. Does DNA hold the keys to unlock the very door of knowledge?

In all Matter, there must be Form. Let's say we have a statue; the matter of the statue is the stone, and the sculpture is the form. You cannot have one without the other. Form can live in a person's thought, but it needs matter to be fully attained by the world. The matter is the DNA, and the form is our thoughts. The spirals, or the DNA, are a bridge from thought to higher spiritual realization which lead us to other dimensions, and it represents evolution of consciousness.

And if you remember from The Tree of Life section the letter Beth is: *Beth's key word in Formation. It forms sounds in patterns. Form as in the formation of a baby in the womb and so is the feminine principle for humanity.* I became aware of a quality/concept, Hope, that people thought I possessed long before my daughter was born.

From this awareness my husband and I decided to name our daughter long before I was pregnant with her, in fact seven years earlier. The thought, the form of hope, was conceived but not her. Did we desire (hope) a baby girl to represent the concept of Hope so badly that we created her in matter? The Matter of Hope. The form has to come first before it can be attained in matter.

It was 2001 I drew the letter Beth. Was it made by the spirit of God or Hope herself moving my hand, wanting me to learn its meaning so I would speak about how this all works? AND the Hebrew letter Beth forms sounds in patterns to form words in black and white on this page out to you.

Beth's key word is Formation. Our thoughts create what we all hope for whether it is a child or an organization toward peace or a house for your family the form must come first. As far as the defect in our daughter, it was unknown what caused the defect. Heredity, my age, or what the doctor described was the most probable: a cosmic ray hit the egg at conception. Whatever it was that created this defect, we still had a daughter by the name of Hope. As with Pandora's Box, the suffering was on the top, but beneath it all was Hope. DNA was the vessel, and with this mishap of mass and nature came the depth of sorrow, and now, with this message at the bottom—more Hope for all. Perhaps it was the message of the soul of our child giving all of us a wake-up call about the way it all works in this world. As the new theory speaks that nothing is random, that the DNA of the universe and our daughter has a message, whether it is that defect was formed from something toxic or from deeper cosmic mind, the outcome has been to keep this concept of Hope alive and communicated to you.

When we lose someone, or something, important in our lives, we have a shock to the system. Our will is diminished. We feel as if a part of us is dead. We have attached these people and events to us so when they are gone, we loose some of our will to live. The vital energy to survive and to stay in the physical life is questioned. At my daughter's death, I knew I needed to do something to change how I felt and make sense of tragedy in our lives, so we could go on living. I knew that it had to be done immediately. No waiting, no thinking. Action needed to be taken, or I felt like I would die.

When she died, the matter of her body and the form of Hope died as well. When we decided within hours to give her body to science, we wondered if this allowed her rebirth and the rebirthing of our family as well. Because we gave her body to science, once again in the form of Hope, was attached to the matter, her tiny body. Even though she died, her matter was still very much alive in the form of Hope for other families. There is a baby, or babies, in the world today who have the matter of our Hope, and there are families who have received new information about DNA defects because of the study of our daughter after her death. And as a result, did we not only keep our daughter alive, so to speak, but it kept the form of Hope alive in those children and families, and in us. And now I trust, in YOU, as well.

Matter must have Form; and if Hope is the thought form, then each child born is the matter of hope. You and your DNA are the matter of Hope. Let the Matter of Hope live in you now and beyond.

Soul receives from soul that knowledge, therefore, not by book nor from tongue. If knowledge of mysteries comes after emptiness of mind, that is illumination of heart.

(Melanoma Rumi)

*The best remedy for those who are afraid,
lonely or unhappy is to go outside,
somewhere where they can be quiet,
alone with the heavens, nature and God.
Because only then does one feel that all is as it should be
and that God wishes to see people happy,
amidst the simple beauty of nature.
I firmly believe that nature brings solace in all troubles.*

(Anne Frank)

Rocky Roads

Recently my husband and I made a pact that we would hike, not just walk, but hike, once a week. We have gone 5 weeks now. Two weeks my husband complained the hike was not exciting enough. I loved these trails, they were gentle soft paths. The second week we went out he wanted to look for unusual rocks and to do that we had to walk through a wash. For those of you who do not come from this area a wash is a dry creek or river bed. In the desert, we have times when it rains very hard and creates creeks and small rivers all over. The rest of the year they are dry and rocky. So we walked about a half of a mile over rocks. He had a wonderful time and found some great rocks for his office and to have in our yard.

Last week we started on one of the trails I enjoy, soft and gentle and as we started; he complained. I stopped him and said, "Let's go across the road. There is a great wash we can walk." Off we went with great anticipation. So here I was in my Dr. Scholl's climbing over rock after rock. Edwin led the way happy as a lark playing Mr. Geologist. I was a little annoyed but trod on. Then I heard in my head the following, "This is like your life with him. It has been very rocky but you kept following him. Now things are the smooth, soft trail in your life, the way you love it. Now he makes you walk the real rocks and leading to place unknown just as in your life in the past." I laughed out loud and told him. He just agreed and kept walking and looking for the rocks.

Here is the point, along the way I learned to walk the rocks so I was safe. I saw so many beautiful things in nature. I wished I had brought my camera. Looking down I saw large rock formations that were like works of art. There were fallen trees that were sculptures. We found an island with just a few trees and we could not stop walking forward. I was now with him and as we looked ahead we wanted to go forth and discover more beauty. We decided to stop and have our pear, water, and peanuts we had in our backpack. We moved on and at one point I said I wanted to stop and meditate while he walked the wash.

The silence was so deep. Birds and insects were all my ears could hear. The silence drew me in. It caused such calm and peace. As I came out of the meditation I thought: "I will take this with me…it is now a part of me." I called to Edwin to come back and told him I wanted to go. We found a trail that lead us back to the road and only a short way to the parking area. This week while in my office working on the computer I found my mind and soul wandering back there. Later in the day he told me the same thing happened with him. We wanted to be there! We plan to go back again and again.

I have had a few weeks of rocky times with my clients and others in my life. Sometimes we are led down roads and paths we do not want to go. As we start out it is difficult and we try to stop but are pushed by others to make us continue. We never know where it will end or what we are to learn from the experience. As I did with learning to walk on the rocks and focus on beauty I learned to focus on what these people were teaching me. I have not come to the end of the trail but the things I have learned along that rocky road are valuable lessons. Just because it is difficult does not make it less, it sometimes means so much more than you expect.

(Taken from "Conscious Living Newsletter" by Alice Molter -Serrano)

Part VII

Nature

Our Physical World as Matter: Nature

**We have emotions because nature itself is emotional,
and because we are inside of nature, not outside of it.
We have a spiritual life because the Earth is a numinous entity,
a manifestation in the material realm of spiritual energy,
a fact recently rediscovered by quantum physicists
but long ago understood by native peoples throughout the globe.**

(Philip Sutton Chard)

Last but not least, nature instructs us about hope. Whenever you walk out your door there is the opportunity to find instant HOPE. The air we breathe, the sunshine, the stars and moon in the night sky, the creeks and oceans, the mountains and rocks, trees and birds, animals and bees are all living proof that life is a miracle. That we are part of something greater.

Religion, traditional therapy, traditional medicine and almost all aspects of our lives since the industrial revolution began has ignored that we ARE nature and a part of it. Henry David Thoreau and a group of women and men at the turn of the century tried to warn us.

*I went to the woods because I wished to live deliberately,
to front only the essential facts of life,
and see if I could not learn what it had to teach,
and not, when I came to die,
discover that I had not lived.*

(Henry David Thoreau)

If ALL else fails walk out into nature. Its beauty, rhythms and non-judgmental essence heals.

I count myself very fortunate and am proud to tell you that I was raised on a farm in the Midwest. Because my brother and sister were much older than I, I was alone while they went to school, my dad was in the field and my mother was in the house. I would spend hours upon hours in nature. In the summers I was barefoot all summer long. I have vivid memories of spending time sprawled out on the ground on my belly watching the ants. I remember sitting under the lilacs observing the spiders spinning their webs and picking berries and climbing trees. There was no sense of time and no worries, the earth told me what to do if I listened and watched.

In the past few years I told my mother how much I learned from her about nature and her reply was, "That was not me. You spent time outside and you learned it on your own with nature." Being a mother myself, I understand that she held the time and space while working in her kitchen or in the house watching out for me as I explored in the safety of our little farm. This is the knowledge I have to this day.

This knowledge is something that can only be learned by being in nature. We can use the largest organ of our body, the skin, to soak up the information that is everywhere in the air, the sun, the moon, the water and wind. The sounds that I call true music: birds, wind in the trees and the grasses, the water sweeping over the rocks on a journey to places unknown and insects busy with keeping the balance of it all. This is the knowledge that is a part of my body and of yours, waiting to be awakened.

Modern man's difficulties, dangerous beliefs and feelings of loneliness, spiritual emptiness, and personal weakness are caused by his illusions about, and separation from, the natural world.

(Benjamin Hoff)

I would say that this knowledge, more than any thing that I have written about prior to this, holds the best motivator in finding hope. There is NO arguing with nature. It is alive and tells us we are a part of it; we receive direct information with no question. We have a very difficult time controlling it, although we try. It is here we learn acceptance.

Nature speaks directly to our DNA. It is a part of the creator as are we. It has written into it the same information but in another language. As with music nature stands in its strength, beauty, and wonder and if we listen we can hear her voice.

Stress is basically a disconnection from the earth, a forgetting of the breath. Stress is an ignorant state. It believes that everything is an emergency. Nothing is that important. Just lie down.

(Natalie Goldberg)

Nature will not let us stay in any one place too long.
She will let us stay just long enough to gather the experience necessary to the unfolding and advancement of the soul. This is a wise provision, for should we stay here too long, we would become too set, too rigid, too inflexible. Nature demands the change in order that we may advance.
When the change comes, we should welcome it with a smile on the lips and a song in the heart.

(Dr. Ernest Holmes)

When I walk outside two of the greatest spiritual concepts leap out at me: gratitude and humility. How can one not feel the power and beauty of nature and not want to fall on your knees in awe? The power of the wind and water, sunlight shining on a mountain, stirs life in me. All of this humbles me. To give thanks for this earth and all it has for us to behold. If we can find gratitude, hope comes naturally.

On tops of mountains,
as everywhere to hopeful souls,
it is always morning.

Many go fishing all their lives without knowing
that it is not fish they are after.

(Henry David Thoreau)

The goal of life is to make your heartbeat match the beat of the universe, to match your nature with Nature.

(Joseph Campbell)

Most of us come onto this earth not knowing who we are. In time, some of us, because of position in life and family ties, think we know ourselves. Many of us search through religion, psychology, therapy, and having gurus who tell us who we are. And then there is the vast population who don't care and live life on a wave like a ship with no rudder. A very small percentage of us know who we are early on.

Knowing who you are is not about learning but remembering. There are clues as life goes by. There are patterns and repeating events and experiences as we live. Sometimes we curse these and want to put them out of our minds. We are joyful and say how lucky we are in the case of good things. Luck has nothing to do with it But if you are noticing these events and are aware of them and their patterns they really are "markers" for us to remember who we are and why we are on the earth.

(Standing at the Threshold of Heaven by Alice Molter-Serrano)

Epilogue

Life Is But a Dream

While the crisis stage of grief does pass in its own time—
and each person's grief has its own timetable
—deep feelings don't disappear completely.
But ultimately you come to the truth of the adage that
"love is stronger than death."

I once met with a girl whose boyfriend was killed in Central America.
She was grieving and it was paralyzing her life.
I characterized it for her this way. "Let's say you're in 'wise-woman' training."
If she's in wise-woman training, everything in her life must be grist for the mill.
Her relationship with this man would become part of the wisdom in her.
But first she had to see that her relationship with him is between Souls.
They no longer have two incarnated bodies to share,
so she had to find the Soul connection.
Two Souls can access each other without an incarnation.

(Ram Dass)

Epilogue

Life Is But a Dream

At this the whole pack rose up into the air, and came flying down upon her: she gave a little scream, half of fright and half of anger, and tried to beat them off, and found herself lying on the bank, with her head in the lap of her sister, who was gently brushing away some dead leaves that had fluttered down from the trees upon her face.

"Wake up, Alice dear!" said her sister; "Why, what a long sleep you've had!"

"Oh, I've had such a curious dream!" said Alice, and she told her sister, as well as she could remember them, all these strange adventures of hers that you have just been reading about; and when she had finished, her sister kissed her, and said, "It was a curious dream, dear, certainly: but now run in to your tea; it's getting late." So Alice got up and ran off.

(Lewis Carroll)

I had wished it was just a dream like Alice in Wonderland. Mine was a real life nightmare. When our real life becomes like a metaphor, even to ourselves, it is hard to stand up straight. It is like when we were small and would make ourselves dizzy on purpose and we could not understand up, down, or any direction. The entire room spun round and round. The only way to stop the spinning was to close your eyes hold on to something solid like a table and wait for the feeling to subside.

I closed my eyes and held on for years waiting for the feeling to subside. Only now I was a new person. It was a strange adventure and curious indeed but it was my life and I had to move on. And I did.

Alice had the realization in the dream that it was "only a pack of cards" and not real, and that they could not hurt her. It was all in her perception and as she came out of it about to wake she had the awareness she was in control. The events of my life were not as serious as I had first thought. Through it all I came to know death and life are but one journey. It was all in how I looked at it. I was waking up.

Don't grieve. Anything you lose comes round in another form.

(Rumi)

I now know why this work was not finished until this moment, over ten years from its beginning. It is because it truly was not finished. Not finished in my head, in my heart or in my soul. The spirits that led me on this journey, who whispered in my ear, writing this work, knew I was not ready to hear the ending.

During those years when my husband and I were separated and I was left alone with my teenage son is when all the information came to me. I was forced to hold everything together for my son and myself, in hopes that my husband would come back to us. Little did I know he was really sent away because I was to listen.

It was during this time that a force deep inside of me had me write this material, and I learned that I was able to communicate with those who have departed this earth plane. One day I heard in my mind "People will be coming to your door to connect with their loved ones who have passed on."

Now let me stop and explain how this happens for me and others that do my kind of work. These ideas or statements I hear in my head are not my own thoughts. These things just pop up in my mind and make themselves known. I am listening not thinking.

I was in disbelief at first. You see, I had done this a few times before my daughter's passing and I just thought it was a brief passing thing, that out the desperate need of a friend I was able to do this outrageous thing. But now I had to embrace it and know it was something I was to share.

While I was pregnant with Hope I did feel there was something wrong with her. I have only gone to see three psychics in my life and one of them I personally knew. I called him to ask what he thought was wrong with her or me. He told me that she and I would do great things together, a mother-daughter project. And that it would be not just for Sedona, or Arizona. Not just the United States but the entire world would benefit by our work. I was relieved at the time but weeks after her passing I was angry with him and it took me years to even trust the concept of psychic abilities let alone in meditation hearing I was to do it myself.

Then one day it dawned on me. He was right; Hope would be helping me from the other side. Never in my wildest dreams could I have imagined such a thing. Sure enough, at my first group meeting with ten people present, she appeared to me as a girl of about eight to ten years old, assisting me. After 20 years she continues to pop in and out at times to assist me with clients.

You see, I did embrace the work, and I am a Psychic Medium with hundreds of clients, coming from as far as Australia.

Maybe, just perhaps, I have made this all up; this new found abilities. It could really be just a dream or delusion; all I know is over the past 10 years I have heard and seen things about others that I could never have known.

Each loss brings growth with it, and learning to handle new experiences and taking charge of your needs is part of the transformative process.

(Elizabeth Berries)

Now, over ten years since the start of my work and this writing, a new thought was given to me. Grief is not a normal emotion. Joy, sadness, anger, these are all emotions inborn in us, but grief is a result of centuries of belief systems and the fact that the veil between this world and the next was drawn. Over centuries, for whatever reason, humans started to lose sight that there is no separation between the worlds. As I have written, it is all in how we perceive things. If you truly believe that we live on in other dimensions, then there is no need to grieve the loss of a loved one. The physical body is shed and laid to rest but the spirit of our loved one lives on. When we grieve someone who has died, it is that we are grieving for ourselves. We are grieving for our disconnection from where these loved ones are going. We are sad for ourselves, not them.

In 2011 I heard the date of my mother's death in my mind and called my sister to come before this time. Sure enough, she died on the date I heard. That afternoon, while resting after a long morning of making arrangements for her body, I heard her speak loud and clear to me. I was lying down in bed along side my husband and told him all she was saying to me. She told me the following: "Oh, if I had known how wonderful and easy this would be I would never have been so afraid." A pause, "I had no idea how great it is what you do for others, and can I help you sometimes?" She then gave me a personal message for one of my nieces which I later learned was totally accurate.

I had very little grief with my mother's passing. I knew she was more than fine and I had finally realized that there is no separation. In fact, for the first time in my life after all the significant deaths of loved ones, I was liberated.

There is no death. Society has ingrained in the masses how to behave when a loved one stops breathing. We have to believe that a horrible thing has occurred. The truth of the matter is if we all believed that we are a part of the SOURCE (God) and that we are not separate, we could feel as I did the afternoon of my mother's passing. There was the relief that she had gone on, out of suffering; the loss of her mind to dementia was no longer present, and she went to the place of unconditional love. WE too are a part of the unconditional love in the body, but we have been taught and believe we are separate. This fact is what causes all suffering and confusion about this plane of existence.

If we are in reality all one in different dimensions there is no death. Life goes on, and all we do is step over a threshold to another kind of life in a new suit of clothing. All of us have the ability to reach and speak to those in the other dimensions, it is in our matter of our DNA and our brains. We are equipped; we have just lost the instructions on how to use the equipment. Plus there are very few of us around to teach the rest.

Eternity is not a long time; rather, it is another dimension. It is that dimension to which time-thinking shuts us. And so there never was a creation. Rather, there is a continuous creating going on. This energy is pouring into every cell of our being right now, every board and brick of the buildings we sit in, every grain of sand and wisp of wind.
(Joseph Campbell)

So after all of this, you are still sitting there asking "why me". Begin to listen. Why did this happen to me? Whether it is a death of a spouse or child too early, a spouse walking away from you, being fired from a career you had for years, or the loss of your home, there is a reason. We are here to learn on this earth. Sometimes we have to learn from hard knocks. If we are able to be still and listen, ponder, be an investigator of your own life you can understand why. Go within with your DNA antenna. Who knows, maybe it happened so you could do totally different work. Perhaps there are new people that are going to show up in your life or there is a need for a new organization to be formed to study some disease or social issue and you are to do that. Or maybe you are just to learn more about yourself and your relationship with the force of the Universe that created us. There is always a reason. Use the tools that I have given you in these pages to inspire and help give you ways to piece the reasoning out. It may come all at once or it may take years but if you want to know it badly enough it will arrive for you. Do your work. Relax and listen. Do more study and listen. Let it go all together and allow it to come to you.

When we let go of our plans, our preconceived ideas of the outcome of everything and allow the ebb and flow of our life to be just that, we can stand back in awe and wonderment about how it all works. The source of all being holds us in the palm of his/her hand. Hope is ever present!

My life, *"It was a curious dream"* indeed!

Row Row Row your boat
gently up the stream
Merrily Merrily Merrily Merrily

life is but a dream

Bibliography

Books

Adams, Brian. *How to Succeed*. Chatsworth: Wilshire Book Co. 1985.

Berrien, Elizabeth. *Creative Grieving: A Hip Chick's Path from Loss to Hope*. Austin, Texas: River Grove Books, 2013.

Bible, King James Version. Cleveland/New York: The World Publishing Co. 1963.

Blake, William. The Marriage of Heaven and Hell. *The Poetical Works of William Blake*. London: Oxford University Press. 1908.

Bolen, Jean Shinado, M.D. *The Tao of Psychology: Synchronicity and the Self*. San Francisco: HarperSanFrancisco. 2005.

Bonta, Vanna. *Flight: A Quantum Fiction Novel*. Merididan House. 1996.

Bradbury, Ray. *Dandelion Wine*. New York: Random House, 1985.

Braden, Gregg. *The God Code: The Secret of our Past, the Promise of our Future*. Carlsbad: Hay House. 2005.

Brother David Steindel-Rast. *Gratefulness, The Heart of Prayer: An Approach to Life in Fullness*. Mahwah: Paulist Press.1984.

Caddy, Eileen. *Footprints on the Path*. London: Findhorn Press; 1991 (third edition)

Campbell, Don. *The Mozart Effect: Tapping the Power of Music to Heal the Body, Strengthen the Mind, and Unlock the Creative Spirit*. Fort Mill: Quill. 2001 (reprint).

Campbell, Joseph. *Flight of the Wild Gander: Explorations in the Mythological Dimension - Selected Essays, 1944-1968 (The Collected Works of Joseph Campbell)*. San Francisco: New World Library. 2002.

---. *Myths of Light: Eastern Metaphors of the Eternal (The Collected Works of Joseph Campbell)*. Novato: New World Library. 2014 (reprint).

---. *The Power of Myth*. Companion book to video. New York: Doubleday. 1988.

Carroll, Lewis. *Alice's Adventures in Wonderland & Through the Looking Glass*. New York: Macmillan, 1865.

Chopra, Deepak. *How to Know God: The Soul's Journey into the Mystery of Mysteries*. New York: Crown Publishing Group, 2001.

Chard, Philip Sutton. *The Healing Earth: Nature's Medicine for the Troubled Soul*. Minnetonka: Northword Press, 1999.

Diderot, Denis. "On Dramatic Poetry." *Diderot's Selected Writings*. Lester G. Crocker, Ed. New York: Macmillan, 1966.

Gardner, James. *Biocosm: The New Scientific Theory of Evolution: Intelligent Life Is the Architect of the Universe*. Inner Ocean Publishing. 2003.

Gurney, James. *Color and Light*. Riverside: Andrews McMeel Publishing. 30 November 2010.

Herbert, Frank. *Dune*. New York: Penguin. 1990.

Hills, Christopher, Ed., Phil Allen, Alastaire Bearne, Roger Smith. *Energy Matter and Form: Toward a Science of Consciousness*. Boulder Creek: University of the Trees Press, 1977.

Hopking, C. J. M. *The Practical Kabbalah Guidebook*. New York: Sterling. 2001.

Jamplosky, Jerry. *There Is a Rainbow Behind Every Cloud*. Berkeley: Celestial Arts. 1995.

Jung, Carl. *The Archetypes and The Collective Unconscious (Collected Works of C.G. Jung Vol.9 Part 1)*, 2nd edition. Princeton: Princeton University Press. 1981.

---. *Collected Works of C. G. Jung*. Princeton University Press. Retrieved 20 January 2014 (e-book).

---. *Man and His Symbols*. Garden City: Doubleday, 1964.

George Lewith T. MA, MRCGP, MRCP. *Acupuncture-Its Place in Western Medical Science*. New York: HarperCollins. 1985..

Khan, Hazrat Inayat. *Philosophy, Psychology and Mysticism, Part I, Volume XI*. Boston: Shambhala Publications, Inc. 1991.

McTaggart, Lynne. *The Field, The Quest for the Secret Force of the Universe*. New York: HarperCollins, 2002.

Obama, Barack. *The Audacity of Hope*. Crown Publishing Group. New York, 2006.

Peat, F. David. *Synchronicity: The Bridge between Matter and Mind*. New York: Bantam. 1985 (reprint).

Ramacharaka, Yogi (William Walter Atkinson). *The Hindu Yogi Science of Breath*. originally published in 1905. holisticonline.com. e-book available: http://www.gutenberg.org/ebooks/13402

Richo, David, Ph.D. *Unexpected Miracles: The Gift of Synchronicity & How to Open It.* New York: The Crossroad Publishing Company. 1998.

Roberts, Jane. *The Nature of Personal Reality: Specific, Practical Techniques for Solving Everyday Problems and Enriching the Life You Know.* San Rafael: Amber-Allen Publ., New World Library; 1994 (reprint).

Schweitzer, Albert. *Reverence for life, Sermons by Albert Schweitzer*, translated by Reginald H. Fuller. New York: Harper and Row. 1969.

Nature of Consciousness,. 8 June 2015. http://www.scienceandnonduality.com

Siegel, Bernie, M.D. *Love, Medicine and Miracles.* HarperCollins. New York, 1986.

Small, Jacquelyn. *Transformers, The Therapists of the Future.* Marina del Rey: Devors & Company. 1982.

Sussman, Janet I. *Time Shift: The Experience of Dimensional Change.* Charlotte: Time Portal Publications. 1996.

Thoreau, Henry David. *Walden.* Boston: Ticknor and Fields, 1854.

Tolle, Eckhart. *The Power of Now.* New York: Plume Penguin Group. 2005.

Twain, Mark, Howard G. Baetzhold. *The Bible According to Mark Twain.* New York: Touchstone. 1995.

We'Moon. *Gaia Rhythms for Womyn.* Wolf Creek: Mother Tongue Ink. 1999.

Wolpe, David, Rabbi. *Making Loss Matter: Creating Meaning in Difficult Times.* New York, 1999.

Woolger, Jennifer Barker and Roger J. Woolger. The *Goddess Within: A Guide to the Eternal Myths that Shape Women's Lives.* New York: Random, 1989.

Conversations, Interviews, Audiobooks, Videos

Greene, Brian. 14 December 2015. http://www.pbs.org/wnet/musicinstinct/tag/brian-greene/

---. 3 June 2015. http://pbs.org/wnet/musicinstinct/video/physics-of-sound/all-music-comes-from-vibrations/56/

Icke, David. "*Sound Vibration Equals Form*" (video) ("Everything Is Sound", Arturo Garces)

McKnight, Michael. "*Elders and Guides: A Conversation with Joseph Campbell.*" Parabola 5. February 1980.

Moyers, Bill. "*The Power of Myth."* Mystic Fire Video. 1988.

Toms, Michael. *"The Wisdom of Joseph Campbell: in Conversation with Michael Toms."* (New Dimensions Radio Interview.) New York: Hay House. 2005.

Newspaper and Magazine Articles

Fromm, Erich, Ph.D. Quotation. *New York Times.* 5 Jan 1964.

Web/Internet

Abraham. The Law of Attraction: Teachings of Abraham.

Adams, Bryan. 3 June 2015. http://www.sapphyr.net/smallgems/qoutes-thoughts-create-reality.htm

Acharya, Pundit. 15 March 2015. http://www.spiritsound.com/sing/breath1.html

Appollinaire, Guillaume. 25 November 2014. http://www.goodreads.com/author/quotes/66522.Guillaume_Apollinaire

Aristotle. 3 June 2015. http://www.brainyquote.com/quotes/authors/a/aristotle.html

Aurelius, Marcus. 9 October 2014. http://www.brainyquote.com/quotes/quotes/m/marcusaure143088.html

Barry, Dave. 2 June 2015. http://www.goodreads.com/quotes/326474-all-of-us-are-born-with-a-set-of-instinctive

Beecher, Henry Ward. 24 October 2014. http://www.quotealbum.com/quote/UrxNQ/good-humor-makes-all-things-tolerable

Beiser, Arnold. 9 October 2014. http://thinkexist.com/quotation/the_tragic_or_the_humorous_is_a_matter_of/184199.html

Berrien, Elizabeth. 3 June 2015. http://www.goodreads.com/quotes/961539-each-loss-brings-growth-with-it-and-learning-to-handle

Blake, William. electromechanical. 11 April 2013. http://www.poetrychaikhana.com/Poets/B/BlakeWilliam/AwakeawakeO/index.html

---. https://www.goodreads.com/quotes/3679-if-the-doors-of-perception-were-cleansed-every-thing-would

---. http://www.blakearchive.org/exist/blake/archive/work.xq?workid=mhh&java=no

Blount, Thomas. 2 June 2015. http://www.spiritual-quotes-to-live-by.com/nature-quotes.html

Braden, Gregg, quoting Max Planck. 2 June 2015. http://www.greggbraden.com/additional-resources/

Campbell, Joseph. 6 October 2014. http://www.brainyquote.com/quotes/authors/j/joseph_campbell.html?SPvm=1&vm=l

---. The Power of Myth. http://goodreads.com/work/quotes/971052

Cicero. 24 November 2014. http://www.quotationspage.com/quote/31217.html

---. http://www.brainyquote.com/quotes/quotes/m/marcustull156324.html

Chagall, Marc. brainyquote.com. 29 April 2013. http://www.brainyquote.com/quotes/quotes/m/marcchagal146514.html

Chopra, Deepak. 15 March 2015. http://en.thinkexist.com/quotation/the_physical_world-including_our_bodies-is_a/260118.html

---. http://thoughtful-mind.com/quote.php/Deepak_Chopra

de Bono, Edward. 25 November 2014. http://www.goodreads.com/author/quotes/6980.Edward_De_Bono

de Lint, Charles. 21 August 2015. http://izquotes.com/author/charles-de-lint

Dennison and Dennison. 6 October 2014. http:/www.braingym.com/. http://edu-kinesthetics.com/store.html

Dass, Ram. 2 December 2014. http://www.ramdass.org/learning-grieve/

Deschene, Lori. 2 June 2015. http://tinybuddha.com/quotes/tiny-wisdom-the-beauty-of-starting-over/

Dickinson, Emily. 6 October 2014. http://www.quotesby.net/Emily-Dickinson.

Douglas, Helen Gahagan. 2 June 2015. http://www.quotes.net/quote/12667

Dusek, Brett. 2 June 2015. http://creativesagest.blogspot.co.uk/2009/03/golden-ratio-secret-to-aesthetics.html

Edmonds, Molly. 4 June 2015. http://people.howstuffworks.com/what-is-hope.htm

Einstein, Albert. 11 April 2013. http://thinkexist.com/quotation/a_human_being_is_part_of_a_whole-called_by_us_the/10110.html

---. 11 October 2014. http://quotespictures.com/everything-is-energy-and-thats-all-there-is-to-it-match-the-frequency-of-the-reality-you-want-and-you-cannot-help-but-get-that-reality-it-can-be-no-other-way-this-is-not-philosophy-this-is-physi/

---. 16 July 2015. http://www.goodreads.com/quotes/1799-the-world-as-we-have-created-it-is-a-process

Empedocles. "Empedocles Quotes." Thinkexist.com. 29 April 2013. http://thinkexist.com/quotation/the_nature_of_god_is_a_circle_of_which_the_center/173078.html

Fleishman, Jerome P. 24 October 2014. http://www.famousquotesandauthors.com/authors/jerome_p__fleishman_quotes.html

Frank, Anne. http://www.quoty.org/quote/4899

Fromm, Erich, Ph.D. 11 April 2013. http://www.erichfromm.net/quotes/.

Goldberg, Natalie. 6 October 2014. http://en.thinkexist.com/quotation/stress_is_basically_a_disconnection_from_the/217136.html

Goodrich, Richelle E. 19 July 2015. http://www.goodreads.com/quotes/tag/mattering

Hale, Mandy. 30 April 2015. The Single Woman: Life, Love and a Dash of Sass.

Harrell, S. Kelley. 2 June 2015. http://goodreads.com/works/quotes/21495970-gift-of-the-dreamtime---reader-s-companion

Hicks, Esther. 3 June 2015. http://www.goodreads.com/author/quotes/30278.Esther_Hicks

Hoff, Benjamin. 6 October 2014. http://blog.gaiam.com/quotes/authors/benjamin-hoff/4783.

Holmes, Ernest, Dr. 6 October 2014. http://first-thoughts.org/on/Ernest+Holmes/

Holmes, Oliver Wendell. 2 June 2015. http://www.quoteworld.org/quotes/6674

Iqbal, Muhammed. 18 June 2015. http://izquotes.com/quote/91367

Jefferson, Thomas. https://archive.org/stream/universityofvirg00culbuoft/universityofvirg00culbuoft_djvu.txt

Jung, Carl. 8 June 2015. http://www.carl-jung.net/

Kabbalah. 15 March 2015. http://blog.gaiam.com/quotes/authors/Kabbalah

Kabbalah Experience. 14 November 2014. http://Kabbalahexperience.com. Hope is a Breath Away.

Keats, John. 2 June 2015. http://www.brainyquote.com/quotes/quotes/j/johnkeats165498.html

Khan, Hazrat Inayat. 2 June 2015. http://sufihealingorder.info/international-training-course/study-materials-seminar-5/iii-healing/

King, Martin Luther, Jr. 7 October 2014. http://www.americanrhetoric.com/speeches/mlkihaveadream.htm

Lewith, George T., MA, MRCGP, MRCP. 2 June 2015. http://www.healthy.net/Health/Article/The_Conceptual_Basis_of_Traditional_Chinese_Medicine/1278

McDowell, Christopher. 2 June 2015. http://treeoflifeandknowledge.blogspot.com/2005/10/sacred-tree.html

McGraw, Phil, Dr. 7 October 2014. http://www.drphil.com/articles/article/44

Miller, Henry. 9 October 2014. http://www.quoteauthors.com/quotes/henry-miller-quotes.html

Mooji. 9 October 2014. http://www.youtube.com/watch?v=BM-2bOdLPCg

National Organization for Rare Disorders. 2 June 2015. http://rarediseases.org/rare-diseases/trisomy-13-syndrome/

Neibuhr, Reinhold. 24 October 2014. http://www.inspirationalstories.com/quotes/reinhold-niebuhr-humor-is-a-prelude-to-faith-and/

Paracelsus. 15 March 2015. http://blog.gaiam.com/quotes/authors/paracelsus

Planck, Max. 2 December 2014. http://www.noetic.org/discussions/open/305/

Pope John XXIII. 2 June 2015. http://www.brainyquote.com/quotes/quotes/p/popejohnxx109443.html

Popplestone, Charles. 25 November 2014. http://www.worldofquotes.com/author/Charles+E.+Popplestone/1/index.html

Ram Dass. 2 June 2015. http://www.ramdass.org/learning-grieve/

Roethke, Theodore. 24 November 2014. http://www.poetryfoundation.org/poem/172120

---. 24 November 2014. http://www.goodreads.com/quotes/332077-in-a-dark-time-the-eye-begins-to-see

Roosevelt, Anna Eleanor. 15 March 2015. http://www.goodreads.com/author/quotes/44566.Eleanor_Roosevelt

Rumi, Mevlana. 2 June 2015. http://www.goodreads.com/quotes/235823-soul-receives-from-soul-that-knowledge-therefore-not-by-book

---. 3 June 2015. http://www.mindbodygreen.com/0-4458/10-Life-Changing-Tips-Inspired-By-Rumi.html

---. 3 June 2015. http://www.goodreads.com/quotes/32062-don-t-grieve-anything-you-lose-comes-round-in-another-form

Rupp, Joyce. 25 November 2014. http://www.joycerupp.com/spiritualzest2006.htm

Sagan, Carl. goodreads.com. 29 April 2013. http://www.goodreads.com/quotes/612894-we-ourselves-are-made-of-stardust

Saward, Jeff. 2 June 2015. http://www.labyrinthos.net/introduction2.html

Smiles, Samuel. brainyquote.com/quotes/authors/s/samuel_smiles.html

Sri Ramana Maharshi. 18 June 2015. http://www.goodreads.com/author/quotes/201908.Ramana_Maharshi

Suzuki, Shunryu. 3 June 2015. http: //www.goodreads.com/author/quotes/62707.Shunryu_Suzuki

Tolle, Eckhart. A New Earth: Awakening to Your Life's Purpose. And the rest of the info!

---. 2 June 2015. http://www.goodreads.com/quotes/33649-death-is-a-stripping-away-of-all-that-is-not

---. 2 June 2015. http://blog.gaiam.com/quotes/authors/eckhart-tolle?page=7

Turner, Lawrence. 15 March 2015. http://www.unique-design.net/library/word/substance.html

Twain, Mark. 24 November 2014. http://www.inspirationalstories.com/quotes/mark-twain-by-law-of-periodical-repetition-everything-which/

Villolldo, Alberto. 18 June 2015. http://www.hearttoheart.nl/nieuwsbrief/nieuwsbrief-januari-2015.html

Voltaire. http://goodreads.com.author/show/5754446.Voltaire

Weil, Andrew, M.D. http://www.drweil.com/drw/u/ART00519/An-Introduction-to-Breathing.html

Welsh Proverb. 25 November 2014. http://quoteyquotes.com/quotes_by_category/p/proverbs/proverbs_sayings_002.html

Wittgenstein, Ludwig. 24 November 2014. http://www.brainyquote.com/quotes/authors/l/ludwig_wittgenstein.html

Shakespeare, William. 4 June 2015. http://www.goodreads.com/quotes/5775-give-sorrow-words-the-grief-that-does-not-speak-knits

U.S. Psychotronics Association. 6 October 2014. http://psychotronics.org/

Walia, Arjun. http://www.collective-evolution.com/2013/12/05/the-illusion-of-matter-our-physical-material-world-isnt-really-physical-at-all/

Weinberg, Arthur. "The Rainbow." *UK Bahai'i IHSP*. 29 April 2013. http://bci.org/ukschools/ihsptext/rainbow.htm

"Archetype." *Wikipedia*. 11 April 2013. http://en.wikipedia.org/wiki/archetype

"Bahos." 9 October 2014. http://eaglespiritministry.com/pd/howto/hcp.htm

"Chakra." Wikipedia. 29 April 2013. http://en.wikipedia.org/wiki/Chakra

"Circle." http://www.whats-your-sign.com/circle-symbol-meaning.html

"Concept of Archetypes." Carl Jung Resources. 11 April 2013. http://www.carl-jung.net/archetypes/html

"Cross." 16 September 2014. http://altreligion.about.com/od/symbols/ig/Geometric-Shapes/Crosses.htm

"DNA." 2 December 2014. http://www.freedictionary.org/?Query=dna

"Hope." *Wikipedia*. 7 October 2014. https://en.wikipedia.org/wiki/Hope

HeartMath. 16 September 2014. http://www.heartmath.com

"Jungian Archetypes." *Wikipedia. com*. 11 April 2013. http://en.wikipedia.org/wiki/Jungian Archetypes

"Matter." 10 July 2015. www.scienceandnonduality.com

"Mandala." *Dictionary.com*. 7 October 2014. http://dictionary.reference.com/browse/mandala?s=t

Mindful Muscle. 16 September 2014. http://www.mindfulmuscle.com

"Prayer Flags." 9 October 2014. http://www.prayerflags.com

"Rainbow." Answers.com. 29 April 2013. http://answers.com/topic/rainbow-1

"Traditional Chinese Medicine." 2 December 2014. http://en.wikipedia.org/wiki/Traditional_Chinese_medicine

"Why Is the Sky Blue: Colors of Light." Science Made Simple. 29 April 2013. http://www.sciencemadesimple.com/sky_blue/html

For further information about Alice and her work go to her website:

http://www.freewebs.com/messagesofhope/

Or email her at: matterofhope@gmail.com

To buy additional copies of this book go to:

http://matterofhope.webs.com/purchase-the-book

www.ingramcontent.com/pod-product-compliance
Lightning Source LLC
Chambersburg PA
CBHW080548170426
43195CB00016B/2712